Latin America: Catholicism and Class Conflict

Latin America: Catholicism and Class Conflict

Lawrence Littwin

California State University at Northridge

DICKENSON PUBLISHING COMPANY, INC.
ENCINO, CALIFORNIA, AND BELMONT, CALIFORNIA

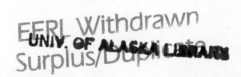

ISBN-0-8221-0117-3

Library of Congress Catalog Card Number: 73-88124

Printed in the United States of America
Printing (last digit): 9 8 7 6 5 4 3 2 1

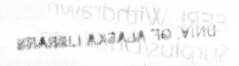

Contents

Preface

This text concerns the historical relationship between the economic and social organization of Mexico, Chile, and Cuba and the Catholic value structure synthesized by St. Thomas in thirteenth-century Europe and transported to the New World three centuries later. This is not a book about the Church per se, nor about St. Thomas; neither is it mired in the misunderstanding that what exists in Latin America today is a stagnant feudalism. Rather, it is a work that assumes the relationships between economic and social organization and a society's values to be anachronistic relationships. Capitalist socieities such as Mexico and socialist societies such as Cuba maintain world views which are a mélange emanating from feudal, capitalist, and socialist experiences. This book will oppose the ideas that a society's view of itself flows directly from its mode of production or that one can determine the dominant mode of production by inspecting a society's world view.

In summary, I will focus here on the survival and even predominance of the Catholic world view through the various stages of class struggle that have marked the histories of these three very dynamic Latin societies.

Mark Roelofs and Frank Morano of New York University deserve tribute for teaching me about the role of values and political traditions in conditioning a people's behavior. Although I have parted from their value determinism, their ideas were the beginning of my investigation. I should also like to thank the war-protesting, vociferous students of California State University, Northridge, whatever their many sins, for challenging some of the naive ideas I have tried to impose on them in class.

Professors James Petras, Harold V. Rhodes, Ronald Dolkart, Robert C. Horn III, Timothy Harding, and Philip L. Beardsley have all read and criticized the manuscript in various stages of its development. I have found their observations invaluable in bringing this work to its final form. I am also grateful to Dorothy Healy for emphasizing to me the works of Althusser and Gramsci. In their sophisticated discussions of the relationship between culture and economic base, I found cogent argument against the temptations of a mechanical Marxism. Victoria Hill, Lise Blumenthal, and Sandy Geideman provided valuable help in indexing and typing. I am also in lasting debt to my editor, Mrs. Jane Johnson.

I reserve final thanks for my wife Susan. Without her encouragement, reorganizational suggestions, rewriting of my many awkward phrasings, insights, and, of course, typing, this book would not have been possible.

Lawrence Littwin
Woodland Hills, California

1

Latin America: Culture vs Development?

On October 14, 1492, Columbus planted the flags of the Spanish crown and the Catholic Church in the sands of the New World. Spanish Imperialism has long been dead, but the values that came with the Catholic Church have survived both this death and the weakening of the Church itself. This book addresses that survival in Latin America and initiates a study of the relationship between these Catholic values and the evolution of economic systems and class conflict in Mexico, Chile, and Cuba. A general survey of Latin American problems and complexities will provide the setting for this study.

The accelerating population growth of a continuingly underdeveloped Latin America would be disastrous. In 1960, 199,235,000 people lived in nineteen Latin countries. By 1970, another 62,665,000 people had joined that multitude. The population of Mexico stands at about 49,000,000, and in thirty years this population will double. If Latin America continues its dynamic underdevelopment, most of these people will lead desperate lives. They will have little to eat. In the worst of cases their children will compete for food with dogs, pigs, and chickens among the mounds of garbage in the dumps. People in Lima and Caracas have seen this struggle between animals and children in the slums of their cities. If the same lack of development which scarred the sixties marks the seventies, housing conditions will worsen. If the countryside cannot provide work and food for the peasants and agricultural laborers, these people will continue their tired but unceasing trek to the burgeoning cities. These displaced *campesinos* will build bigger monuments to misery in the tin shacks of *callampas, barriadas,* and *villas miserias.* Some social scientists have talked of growing urbanization. Another has characterized this deteriorating situation as the ruralization of the cities. Urbanization and ruralization are just words in this context; neither accurately describes the new situation.

The *campesinos* come to the city, but the city does not come to them. If urbanization were occurring, these groups of migrants would be integrated with the lives of the cities. They would obtain the economic, social, and political advantages of urban life. True urbanization would mean that the person leaving the countryside and coming to the city could find a job in the city, use its transportation, be served by the police, the sanitation and school systems, and join the urban political constituency. This is not what is happening. What greets the bewildered *campesino* is a wood or tin shack, which will join other shacks in tight, uneven rows along a dirt street. In winter, the street is a running sewer of mud and garbage. In summer, its dust chokes the nostrils and covers the faces of the ragged little children. These slum towns languish at the edges of the cities. Sometimes they line the rivers or stand planted dramatically on the hillsides as do the *favelas* or the *Loma de Pavo* of Panama City.

The *Loma*, the *favelas, callampas, barriadas,* and *ranchos* are the most dramatic symptoms of the cancer of underdevelopment. Although all Latin cities have their *barrios altos* where the wealthy few live, life for those many permanently caught between the shack and the *palacio* is an austere struggle. Antiquated and often substandard housing crowds many into few rooms with few comforts. Chronic inflation robs what high profit margins have not already stolen from wages.

Regressive Aspects of the Latin American Economy

Agriculture

The demographic tragedy described above indicates that the Latin economy has lagged far behind the integrative and productive necessities of Latin societies. The countryside is beset by poor and irrational land use plus a staggeringly inequitable land tenure system. The United Nations Economic Commission for Latin America reports that including figures for Cuba and Bolivia where *latifundias* (huge land holdings) have been outlawed, 1.5% of landowners own 64.9% of the land. If the two countries are excluded, the figures are even more explanatory: 1.2% of landowners then own 71.6% of the total farm area.

Although agricultural production provides the largest share of the GNP in all but three of the countries in Latin America (Argentina, Chile, and Venezuela being the exceptions), most of this is one-crop production for export and does little to alleviate the needs of hungry people. Given the poor distribution of wealth, the internal market is extremely small. This narrow internal market discourages the production of fruits and vegetables, but motivates one-crop plantation production of such basics as sugar, cocoa, cotton, coffee, and bananas. Thus fifteen of twenty countries in Latin America are mono-economies, totally dependent on just one export item, to which a majority of land and investment is devoted. One fruit producer in Chile complained to me that although more than two million lived in Santiago, no more than one or two hundred thousand people comprised his market. For this reason, his major effort was devoted to the export of his products.

Living conditions for farm workers are deplorable. As of 1969, 42.2% of Latin America's economically active population were involved in farming. Large numbers of these farm people did not receive wages; instead they were locked into bondage to the master through payments in chits, negotiable only at the farm owner's store. In addition, certain farms allow small plots on which the peons can grow some food. However, a charge of 33% to 80% of the yield is placed on this use by the farm owner. Time to work these small plots is also extremely limited with all members of the peon family, sometimes from the age of six, obliged to work long hours under the most arduous conditions for the master, either on his lands or in his house. Needless to say, such basics as food, housing, medical care, and schooling are in the shortest supply. In all of Latin America, the average daily calorie intake is twelve hundred, which is exactly half of what is considered normal subsistence. Eighty-six million people in Latin America's rural areas have inadequate or substandard water supplies, so that more than half of the population of Latin America is subject to epidemic waterborne diseases such as typhoid and bilharzia. Agriculture thus uses much of the population and provides little but the incentive to leave the countryside.

Commerce and Banking

The second most important contributor to Latin America's GNP provides little opportunity and very little income to the bulk of the population. This second most important sector is commerce and banking. It employs 1% of the population and produces 21% of the GNP. Profit margins in this sector run as high as 75 to 100%. To the present, these profits have only intensified the concentration of wealth and attracted large investments into money handling and speculation and away from production.

Industry

Manufacturing runs a poor third among the contributors to the GNP. Its integration and production have not kept pace with either population growth or the needs of the ever-expanding cities. An inspection of Latin industrialization provides insight into Latin *stasis*. First, it should be remembered that industrialization in Latin America has taken place under very different conditions than it has in, for example, the United States. As we shall further discuss, Latin America was and remains a colony. Her primary purpose has been to supply raw materials, cheap labor, and good investment possibilities for advanced capitalist countries. Latin America was initiated into dependency by the Spanish imperium and is locked into that role by the more subtle tentacles of neo-colonialism. In this context of dependency and consequent underdevelopment, Latin industrial expansion merely established another realm of conservatism, stagnation, and regression.

Sao Paolo in Southern Brazil, where industry has grown as fast or faster than it has in other Latin cities, provides a good example of what industrial organization is like in most of Latin America. Recent surveys in this large metropolis indicate that except for foreign concerns, business is run as a feudal extension of the extended family. The *patron* surrounds himself with "men of confidence" (relatives) and retains company stock within the family. He pays extremely low wages, attempts to take inordinately high profits, and reinvests at a fairly low rate. The important goal of the Sao Paolo industrialist is not the success of the business *per se* but the amount of status that accrues to him as the *patron.* He views the national government as a private service to protect him from competition. Although the interests of the industrialists would be advanced if they achieved some common ground of mutual understanding and mutual aid, the personalized or family nature of the business prevents this. Each industrialist tends to view his entrepreneurship as an isolated confirmation of his own power. Therefore, although businessmen may belong to the same clubs and party and dine together, they view each other with suspicion and entertain few uniform attitudes towards the problems of business and its environment. Richard Morse claims that the condition of the business community in Sao Paolo is not one of a class of people, but a heterogeneous grouping of individuals who happen to be engaged in similar activities.

Unions in Latin America

This insularity tends to make union activity very difficult. On the one hand, a primary requirement of the Latin entrepreneur is not ability or achievement, but loyalty. If the worker belongs to a union, he has by necessity divided loyalties. On the other, the schismatized nature of the industrial community makes collective bargaining very difficult. What industrialist A might agree to does not bind industrialist B, perhaps simply because industrialist A has opted for it. This, of course, describes periods when the military is not in power and preventing all union activity.

Most industrial plants in Latin America are not as big as the Sao Paolo operations. The typical plant is a small one, employing less than fifty people. In the two most industrialized countries of Latin America, Argentina and Uruguay, only 13% of economically active workers are engaged in industries employing five or more people. In this mini-factory, relations are even more personalized than in the large industrial establishment. The *patron* can be in continual face to face contact with his employees. Thus proper and loyal behavior can constantly be surveyed. Since the owner of the factory is much more interested in his personal image than in the expansion and progress of the firm, he is also more interested in the sycophantic potential of his workers than in their ability. In addition, there is very little incentive for initiative among the workers because the better positions are reserved for family members, making promotion through merit highly unlikely. As a matter of fact, industrial expansion in Latin America does not imply increased vertical mobility on a merit basis. Expansion simply means "the creation of new middle upper level positions."[1] In many places, Brazil, Argentina, and Chile being notable examples, these new positions are filled either by immigrants or the sons of the oligarchy who, from one point of view, are actually stepping down in the hierarchy.

At the bottom of the industrial hierarchy other feudalistic practices are perpetuated. Neo-colonialism and its correlate, dependency, have not allowed the development of a dynamic middle class. In the Latin context, patrimonial upper-class values rule so that those in the middle class tend to emulate those values.[2] This tends to be so for the union leader as well as for members of the economic hierarchy. The social gap between the union leader and the worker is a large one. The rank-and-file are aware of this and act accordingly. This means that the organized worker has at least two sets of *patrones* in his industrial life. He must defer to his boss and feels by virtue of custom that he must similarly defer to his union leader. The union leader, in many cases, acts as if he had much more in common with the employer than with the workers he leads. It was very disheartening to Peace Corps volunteers I met in Latin America to see impeccably dressed union officials scrupulously dust off meeting hall chairs with their handkerchiefs before sitting.

The purpose of the Latin American union in some ways supports these practices. Given the inflation-ridden nature of Latin societies and their profound socioeconomic problems, it would be of little permanent or meaningful value to organize unions totally around immediate bread-and-butter demands. Instead the *sindicato* serves for the most part as an organ of a political party. Its basic weapon, the strike, is often (but not always) employed as a frontal attack on the political system to gain tactical victories for the party, not economic concessions for the workers. The ultimate goal is touted as the workers' revolution. Party leaders justify the political strike in that the ensuing instability, inefficiency, and illegitimacy of the incumbent regime bring the revolution that much closer. The strike process itself is seen to have great educational value for the workers and democratizing value for the society. This position has a certain validity, but given the non-revolutionary nature of almost all institutional political parties, including most of the Latin Communist parties, this rationale is at times unjustifiable. Strikes which have gained political victories for the Communists, Peronists, and Christian Democrats on occasion have merely subordinated workers to a position they have grown accustomed to. They have been, and in most countries remain, tools of someone else's success. The worker buys this blind, partly because he has no choice and partly because he lives in a world whose hard facts produce the anger and frustration which motivate moves against the system.

It is essential to realize that only a small percentage of Latin workers are unionized. In this case, extremely hierarchical societies are made even more so, with unionized workers constituting a labor aristocracy. The non-unionized workers and unemployed fall below them in the hierarchy of the masses. In that these differentiated groups tend to see their interests differently, organizing the masses to act in their own behalf is an extremely complicated and difficult task.

Effects of Education

Although education has often been offered as a panacea for the ills of underdevelopment, Latin American education has for the most part served as another support of stagnation and regression. Before one buys the unqualified effectiveness of formal education as a motivator and molder of change, one has to consider the following questions. Who and how many are served by what kind of schools? What is being taught? How is it taught and by whom? Toward what goals is the educational system oriented? Finally, how do these goals and the content of education relate to the requirements of development?

Two social scientists studying the content of education in forty countries rated two of the supposedly more progressive states in Latin America, Brazil and Chile, very near the bottom of the list for passing on achievement motivation to their students.[3] This is not surprising. Education systems are basically designed to support the guiding ethos of their societies. An aristocratic society will emphasize in its schools aristocratic and hierarchic values. Except for the occasional rebel, teachers, especially at the elementary or secondary level, are culture bearers and not culture innovators.

In a society where the oligarchy sets the standards for the middle class, the teacher, ill-paid, financially and socially insecure, existing at the margin of the middle class, will try all the harder to gain a secure hold on some status. It is most likely that he will emulate oligarchic values even more than someone with more secure status.

Another important consideration here is that middle- and upper-class children in Latin America do not attend public schools. Their educational track is the prestigious private school. While the public schools inculcate passive deference, the private schools, by their very existence, socialize their students into elite ideas and *noblesse oblige*.

In all schools, teaching methods tend to be antiquated. The teacher is established as a supreme source of truth and this truth is extended as dogma. The student is expected to regurgitate this truth on examinations. However, the university student is the rare product of the Latin education system. The fate of the majority of students, even in countries where a modicum of education is mandatory, does not lie in the university nor subsequently in the professions. Most students drop out at the beginning of the process for a number of reasons. It has been pointed out that Latin American education systems are aristocratizing. They are geared solely to train people for the university; they do not consider the legitimacy of other goals. Thus they violate what might be the legitimate requirements of a modernizing society, i.e., for a moderately well-educated, technically capable people. Since 98% of students entering the first grade will not reach the university, the few years this majority spends in the classroom are almost a waste. If the student has been lucky, he has learned to read and write along with having memorized a gross of useless facts. He has also been indoctrinated with awe for a system that subjugates him. He has been convinced of the virtue of oligarchy and order. Even if elementary and secondary schools were considered valuable for the rudimentary skills they provide, continued attendance is impossible for most. Conditions of poverty are so grinding that lower-class families find it an impossible luxury to sacrifice the potential income of even the very young.

For those rare and fortunate individuals who get to the university, certain faculties are seen as avenues of prestige and power. The law faculties are the most crowded, and medicine is also popular. Other professions have less prestige and some have been deprecated. Agronomy and engineering (to a lesser extent) suffer from lack of students. Both are identified with manual labor. They also presuppose a manipulation of nature considered beside the point and unnecessary in societies in which the rich can get what they want from a manipulation of people and values. The downgrading of technology in underdeveloped societies has a circular effect. Even if a student graduates, licensed in engineering, it is very likely that he will not find a job. Where the major resources are in the hands of a foreign power, higher level technical positions are given to nationals of the foreign power.

The position of the professor also contributes to the weakness of Latin American higher education. What is important to many men of letters is the prestige attached to the position. Many positions at Latin universities do little more than fulfill the status-endowing role. Salaries are small—certainly too small to support a middle-class or aristocratic style of life. For this reason, the *catedrático* (professorship) is merely an adjunct position, a part-time job. The teacher's main interest lies in his profession or business. If the professor is bound to teaching as a full-time job, the low salary forces him to teach at several schools at a time—a course here, two courses there. As a result, he cannot focus his energies on any one position. The serious student in this case is deprived of an interested, available mentor. All in all, Latin America has been bequeathed, by its economic and social structure and by its culture, a group of scholars who are either perpetuating the system or are struggling to survive in it. In that the system is oppressive to the majority, education tends to serve oppression by reinforcing the system that oppresses.

Conclusion

We are faced then with societies that neither serve nor integrate their people. The countryside in basically agricultural societies produces two crops: one is exported, the other is surplus population. The cities provide little more than miserable camp grounds for the migrants. Education secures the bondage of the population.

When I visited Chile and a number of other Latin countries during 1965, the conditions described above appeared to be a picture of stagnation and regression, a hopelessly immutable bind. The rich were urbane and comfortable in a world of servants, big houses, and seaside retreats. They talked of their *fundos* (farms) and served special estate wine decanted informally into bottles which once held forty-dollar Scotch whiskey. They were at once sophisticated, spoiled, and complacent. Their manners and the shell of their life style were emulated by a growing but undynamic, disunited middle class. And always and everywhere were the poor. They were wizened young servant girls from the countryside, far from their families and alone with illegitimate children. They were the workers, the slum-dwellers, and the ubiquitous beggars. They were the majority, eternally oppressed and exploited but seemingly passive and certainly unrebellious.

Where was the vaunted revolutionary thrust people talked about in the wake of the Cuban Revolution? The poor seemed much more willing to annihilate each other than to organize and overwhelm the systems that bound them to poverty. As a matter of fact, where was the reform and development that social scientists in the United States were building models and establishing indices to measure? Population was rapidly increasing. Currency continued to depreciate in chronic inflation. The necessities of life were in decreasing supply.

It was my initial belief that Latin America's troubles were a matter of values. Here were societies which lived within what Mark Roelofs of New York University had taught was the "Tradition of Order." That is, the Latin world view was one of absolutes, hierarchy, and teleology first fashioned by Plato and Aristotle, revivified by St. Thomas, and brought to Latin America by the conquerors—military, administrative, and clerical—who were all feudal Catholics. There was much prestigious support for this position. Louis Hartz's theory of "the fragmentation of European culture and ideology" was a perfect statement of the fact that social stagnation was basically a problem of ossified culture. In *The Founding of New Societies,* he writes:

> There is a problem of traditionalism and change common to the societies studied in this book [United States, Latin America, South Africa, Canada, and Australia], and it derives from the fact that all of them are fragments of the larger whole of Europe, struck off in the course of the revolution which brought the West into the modern world. For when a part of a European nation is detached from the whole of it and hurled outward onto new soil, it loses the stimulus toward change that the whole provides. It lapses into a kind of immobility.[4]

Hartz goes on to say that Latin America is a fragment of the feudal stage of European history. In the same work, the Yale historian Richard M. Morse elaborates:

> Just as there are political and psychological assumptions which characterize Protestant societies and transcend, or underlie the circumstances of time and place, so we may expect there to exist a common ethos within which Catholic societies find their historical development.[5]

For Morse, Latin America "has taken a cultural and instutional fix . . ."[6] Francisco Suarez (1548–1617) was the philosopher Morse credits for the adaptation of Thomas to the sixteenth-century Spanish reality. "His fresh marshaling of scholastic doctrines, under powerful influences of time and place, encapsulated certain assumptions about political man and certain political dilemmas that pervade Hispanic political life to this day."[7]

This characterization of Latin America as a society beset by the ills of an ossified feudalism has other spokesmen, Latins among them. Carlos Fuentes, writing in 1963, called his society a "collapsed feudal castle with a cardboard capitalist facade."[8] Francisco Jose Moreno, in his *Legitimacy and Stability in Latin Ammerica: A Study of Chilian Political Culture,* is interested in change that does not violate cultural norms. Here again we find an emphasis on culture as a static given, the legacy of Roman legalism, hierarchic colonial administration, the absolute but legitimate authority of the king, and the values imported by Spanish Catholicism.[9]

These arguments seemed to drive directly to the heart of stagnation. Latin America did not develop because the behavior of Latins is rooted in a value system that precludes struggle with the science, technology, and hard work necessary for development. Its foci seem cerebral and otherwordly. Feudal Catholic determinism and fatalism reject existential confrontation with a potentially manipulatable world.

Yet for all this willingness to certify the body dead, Latin America defies the grave. Latin America is changing. This change does not seem to be incremental and evolutionary, as some social scientists anticipated. Instead, change seems to be occurring through a violent confrontation between that which is restraining and regressive and that which is struggling to more fully develop and flourish.

Cuba is a dramatic example of this change. In the early 1970s, although the transformation was not complete, the island had moved very far from its legacy of scholasticism, poverty, imperialistic domination, and caudillistic barbarity. Chile, since my visit, has elected a Marxist president and seems on the brink of a class struggle that should radically change a country which the perceptual models seemed incapable of understanding.

In Mexico, agitation, subversion, and armed insurgency developed in many parts of the country in the wake of the 1968 student uprising. Argentina seems to be developing a new and potent left Peronism which threatens the stability imposed by military dictatorship. In Peru, the generals are fostering the destruction of a feudal-type land tenure system and encouraging a bourgeois-dominated industrial revolution.

The Church itself, the alleged guardian and perpetuator of absolutism, oligarchy, and stagnation, is experiencing upheaval. Priests from Colombia to Uruguay are joining rebel units and making revolutionary proclamations. Members of the hierarchy speak for change, justice, and an end to imperialism. At the same time, reverberations from Vatican II have put structural and liturgical changes on the agenda.

The explanation given by Latin rebels to account for the shackles that have bound their societies differs markedly from that given by the majority of North American social scientists and historians. From Castro to Guevara to Raul Sendic in Uruguay, Marighella in Brazil, and Allende in Chile, there emerges an analysis which accomodates Marxism and Lenin's *Imperialism* to the Latin reality. Even the priests and bishops, while not Marxists themselves, use Marxist terminology to formulate their theologies of liberation and revolution. Andre Gunder Frank is one of the leading academic exponents of this Latin Marxist renascence. The kernel of his position is contained in the following quote:

> Latin American societies resulted from the worldwide expansion of "Western" mercantilism, capitalism, and imperialism. Characteristically, this expansion everywhere took the form of a simultaneous and interrelated dialectic development whose manifestations, each both the "result" and the "cause" of the other, are today known as economic development and economic underdevelopment. This capitalist development with its associated exploitation of the "underdeveloped" sector by the "developed" counterpart through the latter's monopoly of force, capital, and commerce, manifests itself on many levels: internationally between the metropolitan and peripheral countries, and domestically between "advanced" and "backward" regions, between the city and the countryside, between commerce-industry and agriculture. If this process is not viewed as a whole—as the dialectic development of a single capitalist system—the door is opened to misinterpreting the results as emanating from a dual system or from two systems—the world of the rich and

the world of the poor—and to the associated misinterpretation of the former as "capitalist" and the latter as "feudal."[10]

This quote is taken from a piece tellingly entitled, "Destroy Capitalism, Not Feudalism." In the same work Frank maintains that the underdeveloped peripheral area "can develop only if it breaks out of the relation which has made and kept it underdeveloped, or if it can break up the system as a whole."[11]

Although I believe that Frank's economic arguments are correct as the basic explanation of Latin underdevelopment, I feel that his analysis treats too narrowly the relationship between world view and the objective universe of economic relations. This book will attempt to augment Frank's analysis by describing and analyzing the dialectical relationship that subjectivity has to underdevelopment and revolution. It will hold Moreno correct in stating that the present is wed to the past, but it will also try to show how the present must modify and finally destroy significant parts of the past if Latin America is to experience a future based on justice for its people.

In the following chapter, I present a model of the Thomist world view with a number of sixteenth-century modifications. This model should be viewed as one of the very important sources of the dominating ideology in each of the three countries studied in this work: Mexico, Chile, and Cuba. As Frank would have us understand, Thomism has not been the underlying cause of events in these countries. However, this Thomistic world view has helped to perpetuate and has certainly rationalized colonial exploitation and underdevelopment. Paradoxically, the neo-Thomistic world view has also served as an ideological base and a subjective context for the dramatic changes that have taken place in these three dynamic societies. It is a premise of this work that if new societies and new men emerge in Latin America, Thomism will have been a dialectical element in that emergence. It is part of the past out of which the future is being forged. It is on this struggle to create a new consciousness that this work is focused.

NOTES TO CHAPTER 1

1. Richard M. Morse, "Urban Society in Contemporary Latin America," *Ventures* VII, No. 2 (1967): 40–41.
2. See Frederick Pike, *Chile and the United States: 1880–1964* (South Bend, Ind.: University of Notre Dame Press, 1965) pp. 284–89.
3. K. H. Silvert and Frank Bonilla, *Education and the Social Meaning of Development: A Preliminary Statement* (New York: American Universities Field Staff, 1961).
4. Louis Hartz, ed. *The Founding of New Societies* (New York: Harcourt, Brace & World, 1964), p. 3.

5. Richard M. Morse, "The Heritage of Latin America" in Hartz, *The Founding of New Societies,* p. 151.

6. Ibid., p. 153.

7. Ibid., pp. 153–54.

8. Carlos Fuentes, "The Argument of Latin America," *Monthly Review,* January 1963, p. 490.

9. Francisco Moreno, *Legitimacy and Stability in Latin America: A Study of Chilean Political Culture* (New York: New York University Press, 1969).

10. Andre Gunder Frank, *Latin America: Underdevelopment or Revolution* (New York: Monthly review Press, 1969), p. 352.

11. Ibid., p. 354. p. 354.

2
The Thomistic Model

The following value model* must be understood in two ways. It is that which ultimately has to change if Latin America is to know a socioeconomic revolution, and it is that which must contain within itself the motivating force of its demise if Latins are to mobilize for and bring about their own revolution. This dialectical concept of Thomism in Latin America will be better illustrated in the study of particular Latin societies. In studying societies such as Cuba's, Chile's, and Mexico's, one can appreciate better the attempt to slay the medieval dragon which has guarded what is at worst neo-feudalism, and at best, stagnant primitive capitalism. In this chapter, I will outline a Thomistic model with its Suarezian alterations. This is done with the understanding that this model is the ideal framework of the unregenerated Latin world view. In that it is a model, it applies to the abstract Latin mentality and does not represent the outlook of any or every Latin American.

This model is also presented with a healthy respect for Ivan Vallier's injunction against an attempt to determine *a priori* the transformational potential of any value system.[1] It is not the purpose of this book to determine whether Thomistic values actually have a dynamic inherency which in itself will bring about the salvation of Latin Americans. The author understands values to be inseparable from the world of matter and motion which they judge. When the world changes or displays to a mind or a collectivity of minds the potential for change, then values accommodate, reject, or modify the change for consciousness. A change in values that is not confirmed by material change or potential change means little in itself. If dramatic changes in the material circumstances and social relations of Latin America are to occur, they will happen as a result of many forces, not as a response solely to the transformation of values. But if values do not change, no chance exists for a permanent and profound alteration of Latin life. Thus, value transformation is imperative, although the Latin American revolution will certainly not be the result of value transformation alone.

With the above qualifications, I will now delineate a Thomist value model so that it can be demonstrated as this essay progresses through the study

*The term *model* is used here to mean an integrated set of values, taken from the writings of St. Thomas Aquinas, which best depict his idealized picture of man in his society as they are to serve God's universal purpose.

of specific societies, which values are under attack and what must change if these societies are to deal justice instead of deprivation to their people.

Greek and Christian Idealism

Plato gave to Aristotle and Aristotle gave to Thomas the understanding that the world around him was the reflection of an idea. Man and his works, nature and its products—all of these were destined to be, for better or worse, copies of an ultimate perfection. Thus, what really existed, had always existed, and what would remain was the absolute universe of ideas. This view is perfectly compatible with Christianity and its medieval experience of gross imperfection and the fleetingly transitory nature of life. For the Christian understanding of history is one that records man's fall and alienation from what God, the absolute, created and saw to be good.

The Static Nature of the Idea

In that God is, was, and always be, the Platonic-Aristotelian notion of the absolute and therefore static nature of the Idea is also compatible with Christianity. Thus, while consciousness may vary, the Idea is constant. So, the life of man is severed from the realm of the Idea. Man can only stand in relation to truth, to the Idea. In that he is in relation to it, he is not coincident or identical with it.

Here is a view of man in which he is sentenced in the context of eternity to a tragic evolvement. Although he can move toward perfection, it will always be ahead of him to tantalize him and will never be realized. Life can be more than Promethean, but less than grace. As Marcuse comments:

> To the Plato of the later dialogues and to Aristotle, the modes of Being are modes of movement—transition from potentiality to actuality, realization. Finite Being is *incomplete* realization, subject to change. *Its generation is corruption; it is permeated with negativity.* Thus, it is not true reality—Truth. The philosophic quest proceeds from the finite world to the construction of a reality which is not subject to the painful difference between potentiality and actuality, which has mastered its negativity and is complete and independent in itself—free."[2] [Italics added.]

Society as a Collectivity of Imperfect Beings

Two inextricable parameters have thus been introduced into the Greek legacy of Thomistic thought: dichotomy and teleology.

"Nature is at bottom a system of capacities or forces of growth directed by [but not possessed of] their inherent nature toward characteristic ends."[3]

These teleological possibilities, which state the inherently dichotomous relationship between the actual and the potential, are conditioned in their evolution by the limiting nature of the material conditions necessary to the teleological development of a thing. For the acorn to evolve into its characteristic and therefore perfect end, it must have the right combination of soil, temperature, and water, and it must have no inherent deficiencies that keep it from becoming a healthy oak. Man creates an imperfect society, and therefore the material conditions for man's development can not be right for the development of his characteristic ends.

Man's Struggle for Survival

This sentence of perpetual imperfection is made more severe by the dependent nature of man's existence. For although the discussion has so far not distinguished *man* from *men,* neither Plato's justice nor Aristotle's *telos* liberate all men from the struggle to produce the necessities of existence. According to Plato, men receive their just due in relation to their calling; according to Aristotle, the difference in the *telos* of each of us allows some to emerge as philosopher kings and others to struggle to produce the necessities of life. *Man,* by the nature of existence, must remain *men* and consequently is permanently separated from the fulfillment of his characteristic end, that of being *Man.* For as long as man is dependent on procuring the food, shelter, clothing, and power he needs to survive, he is deprived of the "joy of being." He must live an "untrue" and "unfree" existence.

This deprivation rests at the core of Aristotelianism and is thus an essential part of Thomism. In order to achieve a comprehensive model of Thomism, Marcuse's characterizing indictment of Greek philosophy is in order. It applies as well to the Thomistic tradition of dichotomy.

> Here, the historical barrier arrests and distorts the quest for truth; the societal division of labor obtains the dignity of an ontological condition. If truth presupposes freedom from toil, and if this freedom is, in the social reality, the prerogative of a minority, then the reality allows such a truth only in approximation and for a privileged group. This state of affairs contradicts the universal character of truth, which defines and "prescribes" not only a theoretical goal, but the best life of man qua man, with respect to the essence of man. For philosophy, the contradiction is insoluble, or else it does not appear as a contradiction because it is the structure of the slave or serf society which this philosophy does not transcend. Thus it leaves history behind, unmastered, and elevates truth safely above the historical reality.[4]

In summary, Greek thought gave to Thomism a static idealism, placing the immutable Idea as the unattainable goal of an inherently frustrated teleology. The whole is characterized by dichotomy, in which the actual is ossified and the possible as ideal is impossible.

The Legalistic World View

With this legacy as his foundation, Thomas built on his medieval additions. Thomas's view of his world refelcts this Greek foundation in that it is legalistic as opposed to socioeconomic. Thomas has little to say, ironically, about how man earns his daily bread. His concern is with the form of government and of law. Thomas, even more than the Greeks, dwelled on earth with his eyes fixed on the ideal of thought, ignoring almost totally the earth supporting his weight. If in a lawless time he was legalistic, in an agricultural epoch his orientation was urban. In that he spent most of his active life in the great university cities of Naples, Paris, and Bologna, he seldom treated the life of the peasant and the serf. This focus on the life of the city as the prototype of human societies was of course intensified by his study of the Greeks, whose thought was molded in the city-state.

Faith as the Fulfillment of Reason

If all the aforementioned parameters of the Thomistic model are heavily influenced by Thomas's Greek benefactors, St. Thomas's view of man's intellectual potential leavens this Greek heritage with a Christian interjection. Thomas, if he is not to completely destroy the credo with Greek rationalism, must set a limit to reason. Within the context of Catholic idealism, this is not a difficult task. A role is written for faith which makes it the mediator between the actual (i.e., the stuff of man's experience and that which his senses perceive) and the ideal (i.e., the product of God's creative nature). In this schema, neither faith nor reason can be contradictory to each other, for St. Thomas's task was an integrational one. Faith and reason are part of the universal edifice and relate to the oneness of the universe in different but continuous fashion. Sabine paraphrases Thomas's reconciliation with Aristotle: "Faith is the fulfillment of reason."[5]

The Organic Unity of Man and the Universe

This intense desire to reconcile medieval understanding, Christian theology, and Greek wisdom is reflected in an important aspect of Thomas's understanding of the universe. Thomas perceived the world as an organic unity. Thus faith and reason were organic or functional as parts of the unity of knowledge. The fact that man needed both faith and knowledge to achieve a full intellectual relationship to the universe was itself a reflection of the functional role of man in the universe. Man's role is to serve God through the attempt to achieve grace. The necessity of two major articulations with the universe, faith and knowledge, underlines man's imperfection. It proves to man that he is less than God.

> For God the whole fullness of intellectual knowledge is contained in one object, namely the divine essence, in which he knows all things. *Rational creatures* achieve a lower and less simple completeness. What he knows in single simplicity they know in many forms. How a less exalted mind needs more ideas is partly illustrated by the fact that people of lower intelligence need to have things explained to them point by point in detail, while those of stronger mind can grasp more from a few hints. [Italics mine.][6]

However, man, less than God, subjected by his imperfect reason to wander through a universe of manufactured complexity, secure only in the perfection of his faith, is assured by the Thomistic conception that his eternal inferiority does not alienate him either from God or the universe. For it was Thomas's task to integrate the apparently disparate. Therefore all that existed was part of the divine unity and, to reiterate Thomas's teleology, all that existed was purposive.

The Universe as a Hierarchy

Thomas presents us with a dichotomous vision of existence, consisting of polar conceptions. At the divine pole is unity and simplicity, the oneness of God, his vision and his essence. At the human extreme, this simplicity is mediated through imperfect reason as an enormously complex order of existence. That is, it is complex because man's reason is incapable of seeing it as a simply unity. Man must work his way back to the unity of God's vision through the maze of Thomas's explication.

The Thomistic dichotomy, with God eternal above and man, temporal and imperfect, below, introduces the hierarchical vision, which is the context of Thomistic complexity. As with God and man, all things are organized vertically from higher to lower. This is true of the universe, society, law, and man's functions. It is to be understood that just as God rules man, in this hierarchical universe, higher ideally rules lower.

In that universal hierarchy is the order of unity, all parts of the hierarchy articulate with each other. This complex interconnectedness presents us with an entirety which is architectonic. Here we have a universe of order, purpose, a great hierarchical whole, in parts functional to this purpose and directly or indirectly articulate with each other and to the whole.

Society as Hierarchical and Architectonic

Integral to this universe is the organization of man's mundane existence. In that the truths of the whole are reflected in the internal organization of the parts, society is a microcosm of the universe. Thus, the complex hierarchy of Thomas's medieval society is legitimated by the hierarchy of the divine universe. The ordered purposive nature of this universe is assigned to society by giving it a purpose and conceiving of its order as instrumental to that purpose. Man lives in society because it is through society that he can answer the needs of his physical imperfection and thereby liberate himself for his divine quest, the striving toward grace. Man's existence in society implies the dichotomous nature of his life. He lives on two planes, the higher one of spiritual quest and the lower, of mundane needs. His nature is both spiritual and temporal. To rule men in their temporal relations, there exists the state. To shepherd man's spiritual life, there is the church. Just as man's spiritual nature is closer to God and therefore rules his earthly nature, in a society the power of the church transcends that of the state. As Otto Gierke expresses it:

> In order . . . to purge away the stains of its origin (original sin and fall from grace) and to acquire the divine sanction as a legitimate part of that Human Society which God has willed, the State needs to be hallowed by the authority of the Church. In this sense, it is from the Church that the temporal power receives its true being."[7]

Thomas and the "Best" State

It is ironic that Thomas, whose major concern was the ideal, the absolute, and the perfect, sought less than perfection in the state. His prescription here is for the best state, not the perfect state. And best for Thomas is always a relative best. That is, the quality of a state was always consistent with the quality of its citizens. Even though the state could be classified ideally in relation to the number of its rulers (the one, the few, and the many) and their goals (wealth, virtue, and freedom) each of the ideal types was subject to variation and corruption. Thus, a few might rule in the practice and pursuit of virtue, but this same few acting as an oligarchy might also have the perverted goal of wealth. A king might rule for the common good or his own aggrandizement. In the latter case, the best type of rule, monarchy, has disintegrated into the worst; tyranny.

This is not to imply that unqualified monarchy was the best form of government, for Thomas's toleration for the less than perfect originated in the Greek sense of the median compromise in practical affairs. The best type of government in the light of this practical sense was a monarchy that included the virtues of aristocracy, wherein the excellent few might counsel (consilium) and the many know the *libertas* of the popular regime.[8] Although Bigongiari feels that Thomas's conception of the mixed government closely resembles Cicero's of the *De Republica,* he states that Thomas sought legitimacy for his plan in the Hebrews:

> For Moses and his successors governed the people in such a way that each of them was ruler over all, so that there was a kind of kingdom. Moreover, seventy-two men were chosen who were elders in virtue . . . so that there was an element of aristocracy. But it was a democratic government in so far as the rulers were chosen from all the people.[9]

In this best kind of government, practical, mixed, imperfect, in a sense a great deviation from the ideal hierarchy of the Church and, in effect, the universe, not all of perfection is discarded.. Although ideal hierarchy would be violated in St. Thomas's mixed monarchy, certainly within this imperfect form hierarchy is preserved and institutionalized. The roles of the various parts of the polity are not conceived of as equal shares in decision-making. The essential pyramid based on the leadership of quality is preserved.

Patriarchialism, the idea of the wise, experienced father leading naive children through this complex life is implied in two elements of the idealized Hebrew governance. The king is the most aristocratic of the aristocrats who shepherd the populace. Thus Thomas has accepted a compromise, a less than perfect situation to handle less than perfect entities in less than perfect circumstances. Humans, tainted by fall from grace, are inherent sinners in their mundane pursuits. These mundane pursuits in themselves imply the necessity of the struggle for survival for less than complete mortals.

Thomas and Law

Eternal Law

Thomas's conception of law provided the link between human government, no matter how less than perfect, and the intricate functioning of a perfect universe. Although all law was essentially a unity for Thomas, it revealed itself to knowledge and faith as a hierarchical manifestation of this unity. In essence, law descended from eternal law in three forms: divine, natural, and human law. Eternal law is primary. ". . . It is ordained by God to the government of things foreknown by Him."[10] It is perfect and eternal. Thomas quotes Augustine: "That law which is the Supreme Reason cannot be understood to be otherwise than unchangeable and eternal."[11] Furthermore, eternal law is identical with God, for "the end of the divine government is God Himself and His law is not distinct from Himself."[12]

Divine Law

Divine law is God's perfect reason revealed to man in scripture. Here we have the divine word, a glimpse for man into divine reason, which calls faith into play since man, through his own imperfect reason, by definition cannot participate in the totality which is the divine conception. Thus, although divine reason is not man's product, it is complementary to human reason.

Natural Law

Natural law is proximate to the human condition and to human reason. It is the fount of human law. It is from man's perception of natural law that he is able to construct laws to regulate his own societies. In Thomas's explication of natural law, one comes to the heart of his reasoning, for both his teleology and the presentation of the inescapable divine hierarchical context are contained within it.

> It is evident that all things partake somewhat of the eternal law, in so far as, namely, from its being imprinted on them, they derive their respective inclinations to their proper acts and ends. Now among all others the rational creature is subject to divine providence in the most excellent way, in so far as it partakes of a share of providence by being provident both for itself and for others. Wherefore it has a share of the eternal reason, whereby it has a natural inclination to its proper act and end: and this participation of the eternal law in the rational creature is called the natural law. . . . It is therefore evident that the natural law is nothing else than the rational creature's participation of the eternal law.[13]

Concerning human law, that is, law promulgated by human kings and legislators, it is imperfect because:

> The human reason cannot have a full participation of the dictate of the divine reason but according to its own mode, and imperfectly. Consequently, . . . by a natural participation of divine wisdom, there is in us the knowledge of certain general principles, but not proper knowledge of each single truth, such as that contained in the divine wisdom. So, too, on the part of the practical reason, man has a natural participation of the eternal law, according to certain general principles, but not as regards the particular determinations of individual cases, which are, however, contained in the divine law.[14]

In Thomas's presentation of the law are the preservation and promulgation of all other parts of the Thomistic model: absolutism, hierarchy, architectonic structure, and, most importantly, as will be seen when I examine the Latin American implications of Thomism, a basic duality between the perfect province of God and the imperfection of man, his condition, and his works. All that is needed is to bring Thomism to its seventeenth-century adaptations to understand its content as an important element in the conquest and creation of Latin American society.

The Seventeenth-century Adaptations of Francisco Suarez

Francisco Suarez, the seventeenth-century Spanish Jesuit, placed an intermediary between king and God and made the Divine Right of Kings at best an ambiguous concept. Suarez held sovereignty in human society to be primarily the property of the collectivity of men who constituted that society. However, Suarez did not contradict the Christian metaphysic of the unity of God. Therefore, this sovereignty ultimately emanated from God. It then passed through the hands of society and into the property of the prince. However, the sovereign power was not delegated to the king but alienated from the collectivity. The prince was responsible more to his concept of justice and good government than he was to the collectivity. In this authority relationship the prince had one major limitation to the exercise of his power. He was bound by his own law. The concept of alienated power and legal limits on its use introduced to the seventeenth century a concept of legitimacy which was to become important, ironically enough, after Napoleon's conquest of Iberia liberated the Creole discontent in Latin America and licensed revolt against the new Spanish throne.[15]

Conclusion

The Thomistic world view incorporates Greek idealism and reason with the Christian metaphysic which emphasizes the unity of God and the complexity of man's understanding and the need for faith. In this combination, Thomas has constructed what was for him a unified world view and a context for the attainment of grace. Although Thomas attempted unity, the overall implication of his work is polarity at best and irreconcilable dichotomy at worst. There is God in his pristine unity. He is one with absolute, eternal law. Then there is imperfect man, dwelling in the cave of imperfect reason and tainted by original sin. Man is mandated to achieve grace, yet licensed to apathy by his own eternal limitations. Thomas has told man that he will always be a subject in the eternal kingdom; that he can never be God, never the master of his fate except in that man can choose among the alternatives that fate has provided for him. However negative these words seem, there is still a positive element. Thomas instructs us that a good political context can create a greater possibility for the achievement of grace than a bad one. The implication is that politics matters and is one pursuit within man's limited control. This work will attempt to explore the tension between fatalism and license on the one side and the struggle to create a context for salvation on the other. Thomism in both aspects will be seen as a major part of the idea structure built upon the proto-capitalist, imperialized base of Latin society.

NOTES TO CHAPTER 2

1. See Ivan Vallier's discussion of S. N. Eisentadt's concept of "transformative capacities" in Vallier's *Catholicism, Social Control, and Modernization in Latin America* (Englewood Cliffs, N.J.: Prentice-Hall, Inc., 1970), pp. 6–7.

2. Herbert Marcuse, *One-Dimensional Man* (Boston: Beacon Press, 1968), p. 127.

3. George H. Sabine, *A History of Political Theory,* 3rd ed. (New York: Holt, Rinehart & Winston, Inc. 1961), p. 121.

4. Marcuse, *One-Dimensional Man,* p. 129.

5. Sabine, *History of Political Theory,* p. 248.

6. Saint Thomas Aquinas, *Philosophical Texts,* selected and trans. Thomas Gilby (New York: Oxford University Press, 1960), p. 4.

7. Otto Gierke, *Political Theories of the Middle Ages,* trans. Frederick W. Maitland (Boston: Beacon Press, 1958), p. 13.

8. Dino Bigongiari, "Introduction," Saint Thomas Aquinas, *The Political Ideas of Saint Thomas Aquinas,* ed. Dina Bigongiari (New York: Hafner Publishing Company, 1953), p. xxx.

9. Saint Thomas Aquinas quoted by Bigongiari, "Introduction," pp. xxx–xxxi.

10. Saint Thomas, *Political Ideas,* p. 12.

11. Ibid., p. 11.

12. Ibid, p. 12.

13. Ibid., pp. 13–14.

14. Ibid., pp. 15–16.

15. For an interesting discussion of this period and the determining importance of the colonial period in contributing to the Latin value structure, see Richard M. Morse, "The Heritage of Latin America," in *The Founding of New Societies,* ed. Louis Hartz (New York: Harcourt, Brace & World, Inc., 1964) pp. 123–77.

3
The Iberian Legacy

The political and social structures of colonial Latin America existed relatively undisturbed for 300 years. The destruction of the colonial edifice in 1808 by the Emperor of Reason, Napoleon Bonaparte, saw the end of political stability but brought the emergence of no new formula to govern the "authoritistic" Latins.[1] Dictatorship, *caudillismo,* and a few recapitulations of colonial authoritism mark these past two centuries of Latin "independence." This history of political chaos has served the developing social structure well.

It is true that the Latin American colonial past has been modified in many ways by the penetration of United States capital and by a certain degree of industrialization. The economies of many Latin countries have shifted from a dependence on agriculture to greater emphasis on commerce, industry, and services. The middle sectors have somewhat broadened to include more entrepreneurs and an imperialist client group. There has also developed a larger more differentiated wage-based working class. Unions and proletarian parties have emerged, accompanying the development of this class. To say that things are exactly as they were during the colonial period would be simplistic and myopic. However, all these changes and many more notwithstanding, a certain superstructural aspect of the Spanish colonial past persists. To say this is not to take a determinist stand on colonialism. It is merely to recognize that in a certain way strong elements of the traditional superstructure have related well to the evolution of Latin societies, persisting with and supporting the emerging class organization of these societies.

Because this Spanish colonial legacy does persist, especially in its Catholic synthesis as a strong superstructural element of Latin society, I feel that it is necessary to spend some time discussing its evolution during the colonial period. In that the purpose of this book is to begin an exploration of the relationship between Catholic ideology and the evolution of class struggle in Latin America, I have perhaps overstated the role of the colonial Catholic tradition. This overstatement was intended to make the tradition stand out more clearly from its very complex and dynamic social and economic background.

Structure of Authority

The Spanish Heritage

Thus, to understand the contemporary Latin life way, one must understand its Spanish structural heritage.[2] The colonial structure of Spanish Latin

America can be likened to a large patriarchal extended family. Diagrammatically, the structure was pyramidal, with the monarch at the apex. Below him in proliferating abundance were numbers of "intermediary" structures. The Council of the Indies, viceroys, governors, *audiencias,* and *cabildos* descended from the monarchy. This pyramid, although reflecting the consistent recapitulation of hierarchy in the Catholic universe, was an ideal contradicted by practice. The ever-present Latin dichotomy between the absolute and the less than perfect actual operates here. In practice, the viceroys, *audiencias,* and *cabildos* were not intermediate to each other. They were competitive units all capable of direct appeal to the monarch. To maintain his power and the stability of the entire system, the monarch played one group against the other, distributing rewards in a semi-pacifying way. However, he had to be careful to maintain a modicum of conflict and competition among these subordinate units to prevent the unity of a potential competing power base. In essence, the king was the father whose affection those below him competed for. As a result, the absolute power (in this case, royal power) was never violated. The theoretical absolute, hierarchy, was legally existent and, like all law descended from divine law, was also inviolate in that it was untarnished by trial. It must be remembered that the king, who derived his power not only from God but as His Surrogate in the Holy See of Spain, was by virtue of divine license sanctioned to be a Machiavellian ruler. This practical license within a theoretically rigid structure is the essence of authoritism and is at the quick of Latin stability. Society is then reflective of the cosmology which is reasonably ordered but ruled by a God who is reason unto himself. The social reflection is one in which not only the king, but all microcosms of authority, have great spheres of freedom licensed by the security of well-understood forms.

Thus while society's schema is a large pyramid, this structure in turn contains myriad small pyramids, each with its own spheres of theoretical reflected rigidity and actual license. A study of Latin society is thus a confrontation between order and anarchy. This dualistic system, which has some validity today, was especially true of the colonial situation. Colonial Latin America had the security of imperial membership, from which it derived a place in the cosmological hierarchy. This membership in the Spanish world gave it the confidence of structure. Geographical remoteness and poor communications encouraged the freedom of authority. The Viceroy of New Spain or the *cacique* of some remote village thus had the licensed freedom to maintain order. His violation of the law could always be rationalized as legal within the license of authority. This is not to convey a picture of chaos licensed by hypocrisy. The limits of arbitrariness were actual as well as theoretical. In that power, in order to be submitted to, had to be licensed by a higher power, it had to be legitimate power. Second, the cultural factor of authoritism implies a psychological dependency. As was stated above, the king was the point of reference, the father who granted to his family. Third, the procedure of power and rule had actual legal checks and consequences, even at the highest level of colonial rule.

Limits of Authority

The primary limitation on any colonial authority was the ability and the practice of the king to intervene and chastise or dismiss the offending official. This might be done on the petition of any individual or group within the colony. This practice kept all eyes fixed on the source of ultimate power. An example of this interplay between governor, intermediary body, and king was the ability of the *audiencia,* constituted as government adviser and highest court in the colony, to check the activities of the governor. If the members of the *audiencia (oidores)* were displeased with the governor or wished to compete with him for power and prestige, they were able to undermine his authority by an appeal to the king. The ambiguous nature of a governor's charge made him particularly vulnerable to this type of power play. However, the personality, charisma, and influence in court of a particular governor would play a large part in his ability to withstand the institutionalized onslaught of the *audiencia.* Additional checks on the behavior of colonial officials were provided in a number of other ways. A standard procedure involved an investigation *(residencia)* of an official's incumbency at the end of his tenure in office. The results of this investigation might bring either praise or punishment for the individuals involved. If a particular question was raised, the king could dispatch a special judge *(visitador)* to investigate in the colony itself.

Monistic System

The system of authority described here is a monistic system with two sources of ultimate power. The one, God, was the rationalization of the other, the king, whose authority was derived from God in the logic of the Catholic architectonic universe. In this entire elaboration from king down through the lowest councilor *(cabildo),* there existed only one constant source of power, the king himself. The rest of the edifice, solid in theoretical structure, was extremely fluid in practice. The latitude of freedom at each descending level of the structure was licensed by the relationship between that official or structure and the king. As the king was to God, so was the official to the king. However, God acted in mysterious ways, but the king could act very concretely. The resulting insecurity destroyed, at worst, or inhibited, at best, collective and individual initiative. The colonial structure effected what it interpreted to be the wishes of the king, recognizing that its acts would either achieve royal confirmation or be voided by decree. Thus the freedom of colonial officials referred to earlier was more in the nature of a territorial charter. It was not a license for political innovation. It was a situation something like leasing a property in a strictly zoned area. An official could be arbitrary in his decisions, but he could not create new forms or institutions.

This characterizes 300 years of political impotence in Latin America. One could conceive of this enormous land mass as nothing more than a great mining venture for the Spanish royal family.[3] It was never designed to be autonomous, to realize its potential as a nation or national entities. It was not meant to innovate. It was developed as a stake in the great Spanish mercantilistic imperium. That it served the economic interests of the *conquistadores* and their descendants, that it served the purposes of the church at the same time that it enriched the king's coffers, only enhanced the stability of the system; but these were not its main purpose. The Spanish *imperium* thus preserved the status quo for 300 years. Once the colonial social structure came into focus and served the purpose of Spanish imperialism, there was no reason to change it and every reason to dictate its rigidity. And the Thomist value structure which rationalized stasis as the social reflection of the universal ideal had every reason to be perpetuated. It was balm to the conscience of the exploiter and soothed the frustrations of the exploited as well.

How Latin Law Perpetuated the Status Quo

As all institutions in society reflect and perpetuate the dominant economic and social relations, so the institutions of law served the preservative function in colonial Latin America. The Spaniards' perception of law conforms very closely to Thomas's idea that the law comes to man in a descending hierarchy emanating from the eternal law and resulting in the laws of man. In addition, the Spaniard distinguished between *el derecho* and *las leyes*. The former is the context of law, that within which the legitimate ruler may operate and maintain his legitimacy. It is the context of law in which positive laws are made. *Las leyes* are of a lower order. They are products of the profane legislative process. Colonial society was so structured that for its every facet there was a legal code and a judge. The supreme judge was the king himself, but below him in the colonies were the viceroys and the governors who had the right to judge certain civil and penal cases. The *alcaldes* (mayors) were judges of the first instance in the same or other cases. Certain attorneys, appointed as the governors' deputies, *corregidores* of the city, and constables all had the character of judges in certain specified cases. In addition, there were military judges, treasury judges, judges of mining operations, of commerce, and even judges of the use and provision of water. Furthermore, the Church, through its *fuero,* existed within its own legal framework. There were ecclesiastical courts with their own judges which heard religious affairs and civil and criminal cases in which priests were involved.

Latin society found a single context of law insufficient to its purposes. In order to rationalize and insure the given hierarchy, a dual context of law was necessary. The law of God and Church were also part of everyman's existence. For the administration and execution of these laws there existed the "Holy Office" or the tribunal of the Inquisition. The courts were at least as harsh as the courts of man. In theory, they were infinitely harsher, for the punishments which they lay down for heresy began on earth and extended to the sanctions of eternal perdition. Thus, colonial law with its two swords, the earthly *imperium* and the heavenly Church, reflected a totalitarian concept of life. Both acts and thoughts were subject to measurement by the legal standard. However, the Thomist syndrome of dualism reveals the ironic nature of all pervading legalism. The counter to totalitarianism is license. Both Thomistic totalitarianism and actual license perpetuate the status quo, the former because its sole purpose is static, the latter because it accentuates an egoism which precludes the cooperation and mutual identification necessary for dynamic change. Thus, the stasis necessary for unchallenged imperialistic control had its own two swords, seemingly antithetical but serving the same master, i.e., irrelevant idealism and non-integrative egoistic anarchy. Both were functions of Latin law.

Causes of Stagnation

The Economic Prohibitions of Mercantilism

The economic prohibitions of Spanish mercantilism perpetuated both the status quo and the value system which sanctified that status quo. The economic isolation of some of the colonies was probably more extreme than that of others, but the mercantilistic ideal was reflected in the extreme. Chile probably represents that extreme. From the beginning, commercial isolation was a fact for this colony. Trading was done solely through neighboring countries or with Spain through neighboring countries. For Chile, trade even with the mother country was a rare occurrence. However, in more prosperous and easily accessible colonies, the relationship to Spain was not so much a trading one as it was an exploitive one. The colonies shipped their raw materials to Spain and paid exorbitant prices and taxes for either Spanish goods or the goods of other European nations for whom Spain acted as intermediary. In the Chilean example, a local trader often had to wait as long

as five years between arrivals of fleets from Spain. When the fleet did anchor
in the New World with goods for the colonies, it usually used the harbor in
Portobello in Panama. Chileans and other South Americans had a long and
arduous wait for the trading caravan. To perpetuate isolation and therefore
preclude the possibility of contamination through the exchange of ideas,
transit to Buenos Aires or from there up the east coast of South America
was closed to the west coast colonies by order of the king.

Trade, and with it communication, was further inhibited by the exorbitant prices charged for goods when they finally did reach Panama. The
masters of the Spanish merchant fleet, taking into account the length of their
journey, the dangers involved, and the certainty of their monopoly, charged
profits of 500 to 900% of the original cost of the goods. In return, the
limited Chilean and other colonial goods were purchased at very low prices.
Because of these trade policies, very few Latins could afford European
products. More important, the low return earned by domestic goods encouraged only a very limited amount of domestic production.

Thus, mercantilism was inhibiting and self-serving in two ways. It contributed to economic stagnation in the colonies and thereby stifled competition. More basically, it prevented the birth of capitalism in South America.
Feudalism, which was being swept away by capitalism in Europe, had no
such dynamic destroyer in the Spanish colonies. One must remember that
the destruction of feudalism and the birth of capitalism were accompanied
by a great ideological revolution. The Aristotelian-Thomistic tradition of
absolutes and order, the organizing principles of Spain and her colonies,
was being shattered from Italy to England. Luther and Protestant thought
were subverting the foundations of the Church whose teachings and repression had molded the Iberian mind. Machiavelli and Hobbes were presiding
over the end of the Aristotelian tradition. The ordered universe was dissolved by these men into a universe of equal, aggressive, and acquisitive
brutes. Chaos replaced order as the basic conception of reality. In these new
conceptualizations, the great growing phalanx of the commercial and industrial middle class were finding the reasons to denounce old allegiances and
sweep away the shackles of economic and social stagnation. The sounds of
their monumental revolution were no more than whisper and rumor in a
Latin America isolated by Spanish mercantilism.

The Church's Inhibition of Change

If Spanish mercantilism is one pillar of this edifice of stagnation, the Latin
Church must be the other. It is greatly responsible for intellectual isolation
and partially responsible for an economic structure that had no impetus to
change.

It must be remembered that the Church is the author of Thomism. It was
within the Church that Thomas found the necessity to wed Catholicism with

Aristotelian order to found a static utopia. The Church, at the apex of Latin society, found Thomism the perfect rationalization of its power prerogatives. If Thomism rationalized the Church's position in the social hierarchy, the king and his soldiers and administrators protected that position. No matter how intense the rivalry between temporal and spiritual powers at the top of this pyramid, the two powers were irrevocably wed. In order to insure its perpetuity, the Church purveyed and controlled this system of thought which allowed no other contender to royal power than itself. It was the Church, through its orders, using symbolism, magic, ideas, and humility, that pacified the Indians of Latin America. These Indians in turn supplied the laboring base of the social hierarchy. The Spanish and Creoles could therefore avoid labor and luxuriate in the wealth produced by the Indians.

The Church was also the sole official conduit of Latin education. They parceled it out in inverse proportion to the size of each segment of a stratified society. To the Indians they gave little more than was necessary to produce docile workers. To the top tenth of society, they made available all the splendor of medieval scholasticism. Thus, nine-tenths of the colonial population lived in complete darkness, deprived of their old culture and the new one, and the one-tenth whose sons could attend the Church-controlled universities existed in twilight.

It was not by accident that the Church established many universities in Spanish Latin America. The existence of these educational centers precluded the necessity of sending rich young Latins to Europe, where the terrible contamination of radical thought lured the young like so many brothels.

When an occasional intellectual contaminant, religious or secular, was perceived, the Church acted through its Holy Office to eliminate the threat. It was not that the Inquisition was so efficient or that the number of heretics executed was so great that prevented an intellectual revolution. It was more the pervasive monopoly on morality and thought that the Church exercised which contributed to the status quo.

Last, but primary in importance, is the Church's economic role in perpetuating social and intellectual rigidity in Latin America. If feudal practices and relationships characterized Latin agriculture, the Church was feudalism's most enthusiastic practitioner. The Church, because of its important role as pacifier and colonizer, was rewarded with a large portion of the land and labor it colonized. The Catholic Church rapidly became one of the major landholders in Latin America. In the colonial period its holdings were tax-exempt. The Church's economic power did not end with its lands, however. Although the Church did not pay taxes, its parishioners were taxed by the Church. This taxation went beyond the tithe. It was considered anti-religious to die and not will the Church part of one's legacy. While the royal power controlled the mineral wealth of the colonies, the Church quickly came to control a major portion of whatever other wealth could be derived from Latin soil and society. With enormous capital accumulating, the Church not only maintained and enhanced its political power but also came to be one of the major controlling factors in determining the non-evolution of the Latin economy and all social and intellectual factors that flow from that control.

Here, then, is a society in which 90% of the people had nothing at all and the remaining 10% had a modicum of economic power greatly limited by the imperialism of the crown and the feudal repression of the Church. This tandem inhibition of dynamism and evolution lasted for 300 years.

Geographical and Environmental Aspects of Isolation

If king and Church prevented Latin America from realizing the consequences of capitalism's revolution and intellectual explosions, nature was no more cooperative. Geography, climate, and a generally inhospitable environment were also obstacles. Given the primitive nature of seventeenth-century transportation and the low level of technical and scientific development of that period, that Latin America was settled at all is a tribute to something in the Iberian character. Yet even this indomitable character had to be well suited for provincialism, given a geography that isolated and a surfeit of natural problems that frustrated attempts at mastery of the environment. Geographic barriers to communication and trade are quickly seen in three outstanding features of the Latin land surface. One is the Andes chain that extends 4,000 miles down the interior of South America from its Caribbean extension in Columbia to the frontier of the Antarctic Sea in Tierra del Fuego. Two hundred miles wide, in some places 400 miles wide, the Andes include some of the world's highest peaks. Mount Aconcagua in Argentina rises to 22,835 feet. Thirteen other peaks reach a grey, frozen bleakness of over 21,000 feet. The mountain passes for the most part are at 10,000 feet or more. In the winter, heavy snows block all passage; in the spring, floods and washouts are common. Geologically young and wild rivers cleave many segments of these mountains, so that west is not only inaccessible to east, but north is separated from south. As a result, many people of the Andes live on mountain islands. In addition, these young mountains are vigorous—they move. Earthquakes and slides happen often, taking the lives of mountain dwellers. There has been some discussion of the impact of catastrophe on the psyche of the Andean population. William Lytle Schurz draws this picture:

> Mass hysteria and paroxysms of terror are often followed by a state of fatalism and resignation. The hypertension of panic may result in outbursts of fanatical religious fervor or end in downright madness as the mind breaks from the memory of horrors and the suspense of waiting for the repetition of disaster.[4]

Whether this is overdrawn or not, it makes a point. Given certain emphases of the Thomist value structure, like the static and eternal domination of God, this unstable and overpowering environment would have an enormous confirming impact on stabilizing these values. Life becomes a matter of *"si Diós quiera."* Isolation as a condition of existence over which individuals and communities have no power is made even more real by nature's constant attacks on man in lonely, undefended outposts.

Although Latin America as continent, isthmus, and islands fronts the ocean for thousands of miles, much of this coast is unhospitable to ships. This is especially true on the west coast of Middle and South America. The ports that do exist—Acapulco, Buenaventura, Callao, Antofagasta, Valparaiso—are not endowed with natural roadsteads. Ships using these ports must depend upon lighterage facilities or artificial harbors. The east coast, however, has two excellent harbors. One is Rio de Janeiro and the other is at the estuary of La Plata River. Two natural factors limit the usefulness of the Rio harbor, and historical reasons prevented full use of the La Plata harbor in the colonial period. One limitation on the value of Rio's harbor for the rest of the continent is the Great Escarpment, which rises to a height of 10,000 feet behind the port city. Trains that make the ascent from Rio to the interior can do so only with the aid of cables. The second limitation on this harbor as a port of entry is the very vastness of Brazil itself. During the colonial period, this vastness was magnified many times by the primitive nature of transport. As was pointed out above, the La Plata port's usefulness as a port of entry for stimulating trade or contaminating ideas was checked by the Crown's prohibition of communication and trade between east and west in South America.

A group of other natural barriers to communication beset Latin America. Among them are rivers that are most non-navigable. On the west coast they are short and tumble into the sea. In the interior of the continent, they are uneven in their use—raging here, sluggish, shallow, and meandering there. Deserts and semiarid areas have repelled settlers and defied travelers. These are the dry areas of northern Mexico, the *llanos* of Colombia and Venezuela, the *coatinga* of northeastern Brazil and northwestern Argentina, and the forbidding Atacama of northern Chile, where in some areas there has not been one drop of rain in recorded history. On the other hand, some areas suffer the deluge. These are the *selvas,* "where the few trails lead like dark caverns into the mysterious unknown and every step makes a pool in the boggy ground."[5] These areas, with their leached soil, impenetrable forests, insects and snakes, heat and rain, make passage (much less settlement) almost impossible. And Latin America has a greater amount of tropical rain forest than any other continent.

One must remember that these geographic factors of isolation are lasting features of the Latin environment. Although the Bourbons were swept from the shore by Napoleon, and the Latin American revolutionaries wrenched themselves free of the remnants of isolating Spanish rule, they did not destroy the mold of their geography. Thus, what was planted and nurtured by 300 years of colonial rule could not suddenly perish. Geographic isolation was not much less of a fact in 1811 than it was in 1810, and it is not much less today. Donald Dozer, writing in 1962, elaborated on Baron Alexander von Humboldt's statement of the early nineteenth century that Latin Americans were "ragged beggars sitting on benches of gold."[6] Dozer goes on to detail the wealth of Latin America:

> Brazil has a capacity for electric power production which is the fourth largest in the world. Chile's copper reserves are more than one-third of the world's total, and her copper production is being rivaled by that of Peru. Colombia has rich salt deposits at Zipaquira which are extraordinary for being several hundred feet thick and covering several hundred square miles. Brazil, Venezuela, and all the Andean countries of South America from Colombia to Chile have rich iron resources. Cuba's iron deposits are estimated at 3.5 billion tons. Ecuador possesses over 90,000 square miles of virgin forest, rich in dyewoods, balsa wood, cinchona trees, and other valuable timber; and Brazil's forest lands in the Amazon Basin include some 1,500 different varieties of hard woods and cover over one million square miles.[7]

Dozer then concludes, "But Latin America remains largely undeveloped. Its natural resources have scarcely been touched."[8]

Social Structure as a Perpetuator of Thomism

If economics, politics, and geography supported isolation and nurtured the growth and health of Thomism, social structure is the immediate vehicle of its transmission. The family and society must reflect and perpetuate the culture or the culture changes. Since neither economics, politics, nor geography required more from society than support, a discussion of Latin colonial society will complete the depiction of a well-integrated universe, discovered and perpetuated for the stability that supported exploitation.

Colonial Latin society, although in some ways more fluid than the society of Spain, more than reflected the clearly delineated hierarchy of the mother country. For in Latin society an extra factor was added to the evolved hierarchy of the of the peninsula: this was the factor of race. For the Latin mind, diagrammatic and legalistic, believing that that which is perceived is perceived partly because a law recognizes its existence, legislated the behavior of the races toward each other. Whereas North American society in its pragmatic lack of sophistication established only a gross black and white dichotomy, or in certain areas a red, yellow, or brown distinction, Latins realized subtle differentiations based on amount of racial mixture and cultural adaptation, and society soon arranged itself into a very baroque hierarchy of wealth, culture, and shade. At the outset, severe social differentiation was a given in this most recent extension of a hierarchical universe. The Spanish came as conquerors. The Indians, many of whom had previously dwelled in their own rigid hierarchies, were the conquered. So immediately, a system of at least two classes was established.

In that the conquerors did not arrive in the new land to labor, but rather to exploit land and labor, the perpetuation of class was inevitable. The Spaniards were to be a non-laboring aristocracy and the Indians, as long as they lasted, were to be the great laboring base of this initially simple social pyramid. However, in that the Spanish king was not about to germinate a competing power base in the Americas, he did two things to complicate the social hierarchy. First, he initiated centralized control by sending out from Spain his representative administrators and bureaucrats to whom the *conquistadores* had to submit. These administrators were rotated back and forth from Spain, but they almost always had to be native born *peninsulares.* The sons of the *conquistadores,* and worse still, the grandsons, were kept at a distance from the machinery of state. Their wealth was great in proportion to their miniscule political power. In the colonial social hierarchy, these *criollos* occupied an inferior station. The second step taken by the king, or at least sanctioned by his seal, was the passage of numerous laws which defined the use of Indian labor, *ipso facto* establishing the legal existence of Indians as a class of laborers. Again, this was done to maintain domination of the given and emerging Latin population in the hands of the king. These laws, when they could be executed, were fairly effective and probably saved many Indian populations from extinction. However, they legally defined the base position in the hierarchy. The existence of *mestizos,* for whom there were no laws, merely elaborated the class structure. It must be remembered that the cultural and racial category, *mestizo,* is itself a tribute to a complex view of social structure. The *mestizo* is not always a racially mixed person. He may be a racial Indian who has "transcended" his particular cultural rung and moved up by accepting the Spanish language, Catholicism, Spanish dress, occupation, and living style. Here we see that social stratification is more than racial differentiation. It is a reflection of a superordinate, subordinate view of culture itself. That is, hierarchy in this case does not rest in the human himself, but in the idea of culture. As always in Thomistic thought, the idea takes precedence over the actual.

What started out as a superficial two-class system quickly elaborated itself into a gross four-class society: *peninsulare, criollo, mestizo, indio.* This elaboration is gross in that it does not consider the inherent distinctions within and among those four groups (such as office, wealth, or family) or the developing distinction between rural and urban populations.

When the Indian populations of tropical areas were depleted by culture shock, exploitive hard labor, and disease, a new dimension was added to the already complicated social hierarchy. This was the black dimension, as slaves were imported from Africa to flesh out the labor supply. In that the sexual color line has never been very sharp, the class picture was soon further complicated by the recognition of different shades of blackness and whiteness. A mulato class soon emerged, and manumission as a reward for various services was fairly common. Thus, within the black population, a small hierarchy developed separating free black from slave. In any event, blacks formed the solid bottom of the Latin social pyramid. Color is not the total explanation for the establishment of this social base. Whereas the American Indians were sanctified in Catholic perception by their existence as part of large communities, discovered intact, the black slave was introduced to the New World bereft of any social context. He was imported as an individual, without society, without family. He was a black atom, a lonely object to which the Spanish Catholic mind could not credit more than sub-humanity. Humanity, for a Thomist, was a function of a category of society. This understanding of the black position was indeed a handy counter to the legislation, structure, and compassion which prevented the total dehumanization of the Indian through exploitation.

Conclusion

This discussion of the political organization, law, geography, and social structure of colonial Latin America has shown the necessary marriage and maintenance of a Thomistic ideology with the needs and interests of those whose design was to exploit and benefit from the exploitation of Latin America. While the *conquistadores* arrived in the New World to make their fame and fortune, to enhance their life chances in a way they could never have done in a stagnant Spain, they came sanctified by the mission of extending the Catholic universe. This mission not only aided the *conquistadores* and the Church, but it also gave the New World continuity with the structures, forms, and mentality of the mother country. In this way, the primary purpose of these newly discovered lands—to serve the Spanish throne—was enhanced. The Spanish kings, consistent in the application and perpetuation of ideological justification, aided by their ally-enemy, the Church, were able to practice Machiavellian manipulation and maintained a relatively stable situation for 300 years.

It should be remembered that it was Napoleon, not the colonial *criollos,* who began the overthrow of Spanish imperialism. Some commentators believe that were it not for the Napoleonic sweep of Iberia, the Spanish colonial relationship might have continued *ad infinitum.* That is to say, that power differentials, dissatisfaction, and other revolutionary ingredients had not come to a climactic focus by 1808. Although there were obviously disagreements, periods of violence, and interstructural and interclass rivalries, in the main the monistic power situation and its inextricable concommitant, divine justification of the status quo, served the elite forces well enough to maintain the system. An indication of the satisfactory nature of this system is that there were no profound or elaborate changes after Napoleon's deposition of the legitimate Spanish throne. The major problem after the wars of independence, and this was no mean problem, was how to relegitimize political power so as not to jeopardize the satisfying economic and social situation of the *status quo ante bellum.* What the *criollo* barons wanted was to assume the political positions previously monopolized by *peninsulares* and thus solidify their own hold over their destinies. Their rebellion was not a middle-class effort. It was not like the revolutionary struggles of the thirteen colonies and the French middle-class attack on the remnants of feudalism. The Spanish colonies contained, in fact, no significant Spanish Catholic middle class. Three hundred years of monistic mercantilism had thwarted that development. The consequences of a landed baronial class assuming power after the departure of Spanish imperialism have been most profound for Latin America.

For one thing, the Spanish New World continued the economic dependence of colonial status long after it had achieved political independence. The colonies-turned-nations maintained their role as providers of agricultural products and mineral raw materials for Europe and the United States. In turn, the former Spanish dependencies served as markets for European industrial products. Their hunger for finished goods and their own inability to produce them were an early drain on Latin capital, which could rarely be redirected into their own economies. When capital was needed, even to finance new primary resource development, this capital had to come from foreign sources. Latin America was thus destined to go from one dependency to another equally insidious dependency. The new dependent relationship was a result not only of lack of finance capital, but also of other weaknesses inherited from the centuries of Spanish domination.

The profound lack of political skills and the particularistic legacy of internal non-integration constituted a post-independence situation of terribly unstable geographic and political isolates. These chaotic, proto-rational units were left to struggle within themselves through a series of *caudillos* and revolutions to attain stability, still an illusory goal for most Latin American countries. They were also the legacies of extremely indeterminate geographic boundaries. For this reason they were to struggle with each other politically, if not militarily, for many years to come. These unstable isolates were again prey to the needs of dynamic and expanding European capital. European and North American capitalists found easy allies among the warring factions in these new nations. For the capitalists it was not a matter of divide and conquer, because the divisions were provided by the disintegration of Spanish monistic rule.

In this way, the situation in Latin America has remained potentially and actually chaotic, certainly not undynamic, yet profoundly stultified. In most countries, the original barons have maintained limited economic power or have surrendered it to an equally exploitable set of barons who maintain the shaky status quo as handmaidens to the real economic control of foreign capital. This foreign control is direct, as in the ownership of a country's primary resources, and indirect, as in the control of the market in which these resources are to be sold. As they were during the colonial period, the Latin nations are caught in a game which they do not and cannot control.

Although this new dependency made changes in the basic economic and social structure of the former colonies, Thomism remained the primary world view of Latin society. Its emphasis on hierarchy, organicism, and architectonic nature of society and the universe, and its complex interpretation of law served to "legitimize" in the eyes of the dominating classes the correctness of their continued domination. This is not to imply that Thomism as ideology was uniformly acceptable. The Catholic conception of the universe and the Church itself were severely attacked during the nineteenth century. This was for a number of reasons.

First, Latin intellectuals, many of whom were European educated, recognized the lagging nature of Latin development, especially in light of Europe's industrial leap. Just as Europe's industrial goods and creative advances were readily marketable in Latin America, so were her intellectual discoveries. If French positivism seemed to be the necessary accompaniment to modernization, then why not apply the principles of positivism to Latin society to prompt development. If the rational use of humans and technology challenged the medieval hold of the Church, then down with the Church.

Second, new middle groups, limited in size and outlets for their ambitions, did emerge. Catholic values and the Church itself seemed the major bulwark of the old landed aristocracy. These new groups had to challenge the old in order to gain the freedom to realize their ambitions. Thus there emerged in many Latin nations extremely anticlerical parties. The ideological input for these parties was supplied by a growing Masonic movement, with its faith in man and reason as opposed to Church and faith.

The third challenge to the old world view was inherent in the nonrealization of Thomism. Although many of the old feudal forms remained, transferred from *latifundia* to factory, the participants were increasingly corrupted and unmindful of their feudal obligations. The poor remained wretchedly so. Most political systems found stability only in the injustices of *caudillismo,* becoming corrupt tyrannies instead of just monarchies. Meanwhile, the rich paid less and less attention to their lands as they found commercial opportunities in the cities. Land was for prestige, and commerce was for capital.

The fourth challenge emerged later. The growing socialization of the means of industrial production, accompanied by socialist stirrings in Europe, prompted proletarian awareness among growing segments of the labor force and certainly a challenge to the old hierarchical notions of society.

In spite of these very real challenges, revolutionary ideologies in themselves, whether middle class or proletarian, were not enough to break the trap of mono-economic dependency and a continued feudal world view. The perpetuation of old forms in turn perpetuated the correctness of the old values. The resultant tandem relationship maintained its stranglehold. In the next three chapters, the combat between the irrepressible new and the terribly resistant old will be explored in three countries where the conflict has been most intense: Mexico, Chile, and Cuba.

NOTES TO CHAPTER 3

1. This author feels that the term "authoritistic" as developed by Francisco Jose Moreno in his work, *Legitimacy and Stability in Latin America: A Study of Chilean Political Culture* (New York: New York University Press, 1969), p. 24, is a more applicable term than the more often used "authoritarian." As Moreno explains, "the term authoritarian implies some element of illegitimacy, and its application to the Spanish colonial system has obscured the fact that royal predominance was psychologically accepted and legally sanctioned," p. 23. Authoritism means "the existence of a single center of legitimate political power, the legal supremacy of which is sanctioned in the name of justice and whose actions are, therefore, not to be bound by written regulations or existing customs."

2. Moreno's work contains an excellent description and analysis of Spanish colonial structure. See also Donald Marquand Dozer, *Latin America: An Interpretive History* (New York: McGraw-Hill Book Company, 1962), pp. 99–123.

3. Historians, like Dozer, maintain that the Spanish Crown was motivated by the prestige as well as the wealth of empire. The distinction seems truistic, since prestige is derived from wealth. The Crown would have gained little from having the imperial flag fly over a mass of unproductive land. In fact, the expense of such a barren empire would have quickly eroded the prestige immediately gained by the conquest. See Dozer, *An Interpretive History,* pp. 25–58.

4. William Lytle Schurz, *This New World: The Civilization of Latin America* (New York: E. P. Dutton and Co., Inc., 1954), p. 30.

5. Dozer, *An Interpretive History,* p. 5.

6. Ibid. p. 4.

7. Ibid. It should be pointed out that although Brazil's forest resources are promising, they have not yet been shown to be commercially rich.

8. Ibid.

4
Mexico: From Revolution to Corporate State

The Mexican revolution has never wholeheartedly struggled against a regressive Catholic consciousness. Paradoxically, Mexican revolutionaries have always managed to elevate and resurrect the past. In art, this resurrection has been healthy in that the great Indian past has been synthesized with the struggles of its Indian present. Ideologically, the preservation of Catholicism in its most obfuscating,superstitious, and rationalizing forms is the sign and method of an unjust system of class hierarchy. Ironically, this Catholicism is preserved, never called by name, while the Church itself has almost been destroyed as a power.

In the long struggle for political power and the resolution of class antagonism, Catholicism played no mean part. Although this study concentrates on men, politics, and social class, Catholicism as a major contributor to the Mexican idea structure will always be in the background and frequently come to the fore.

Poverty and Deprivation

Mexico, like much of the third world, is potentially rich but actually poor. Its population growth is phenomenal and unevenly distributed. Mexico City grows and grows under the weight of displaced *campesinos.* The population of that city has grown from 1.4 million in 1940 to 4 million by the mid-1960s. The exploited wealth of the country is very unevenly distributed. About half of the population, the bottom 50%, compete for 15% of the national income, while some reports place 66% in the hands of 1% of the population.[1]

After sixty-two years of revolution, the Mexican economy is again heavily infiltrated by American capital. The 1962 figure quoted by Andre Gunder Frank was more than one billion dollars, or about one-tenth of U.S. investment in Latin America. Frank goes on to report that:

> In 1953, of the thirty-one companies with a gross annual income exceeding 100 million pesos, nineteen were U.S.-owned or controlled. ... Moreover, since the ownership certificates of Mexican enterprises are bearer and not name bonds and shares, and since after issuance

these certificates typically tend to gravitate into the hands where capital is already concentrated, it is not always easy to determine where ownership, and particularly control, lies. Thus, U.S. control of Mexican industry today may well be close to 50 percent.[2]

Luis Cecena and others, describing the situation in the 1960s, indicate that North American control has greatly increased. They place U.S. control at 60–80% of industry and total control of the largest industries outside of oil and the railroads. Mexican agriculture, agrarian reform notwithstanding, is not immune to U.S. control. Mexico's major export crop is cotton. In that the production of cotton from sowing to shipping is floated on huge credit grants from the American cotton monopoly, Anderson and Clayton, Mexico's ability to determine the market and price her cotton is minimal. Also, as a result of the ready capital reward for cotton, northern Mexico finds itself in a typical third world economic mono-culture.[3]

Pablo Gonzalez Casanova characterizes Mexico's revolution as semi-capitalist. He credits this semi-capitalist revolution with the destruction of the semi-feudal plantation system. It has given impetus to business and initiated industrialization.

> But . . . the country has not created heavy industry nor attained economic, political, and cultural independence for Mexico. It depends to a great extent for the supply of its means of production on the United States. Its capacity for participating in world economic competition is menaced by the great powers, especially United States capital. It imports principally manufactured products and exports raw materials. It has a single foreign market that is predominant: the United States. Its domestic market corresponds to the early phases prior to full capitalist development, and its culture is typically heterogeneous.[4]

Although Mexico has taken huge strides in infrastructural and industrial development since 1910, the figures that reflect distributive justice—the health, welfare, education, and participatory ability of the bulk of the population—are regressive. The estimated crude death rate for 1965–1970 of 8.9 is higher than that of Panama, Venezuela, and El Salvador. The infant mortality rate of 63.1 per thousand births is higher than Nicaragua's. Nor are there enough doctors; there is only one doctor for every nineteen hundred people. This doctor/population ratio is less than half of Argentina's.

Mexico's illiteracy rate is extremely high. In 1960, 37.8% of the population fifteen years and older could not read. Although a little more than half of the population begins school, only 7.4% complete primary school and only 1.6% attend the university. A per capita income of $395 places Mexico high on the list of twenty nations, although well below Venezuela's $800 and Argentina's $530. Of course, the per capita income of Mexico's northern neighbor is over $2,000, and the per capita income tells little about the distribution of this income, especially as it is distributed sectorally and regionally.

Pablo Gonzalez Casanova tells us the following about income distribution:

> An average income per family for the whole country of 700 pesos per month (fifty-six dollars) was barely enough to satisfy the minimal requirements for food, clothing, shelter, and entertainment in 1956, and according to this standard, thirty-three percent of the families in the Federal District and the Pacific North, sixty percent of Gulf Coast families, and those living in North Central states, and eighty percent of those living in the center of the country and in states along the Southern Pacific coast were lacking in economic means to care for their minimum needs.[5]

Gonzalez quotes Ifigenia Navarrete:

> ... approximately two out of every three families were lacking in economic means in the sense of having a below average income, which average itself was already low.[6]

The economic deprivation is reflected in F.A.O.'s finding that the average Mexican diet shows a caloric deficit of 24.4 calories.

These rather depressing figures are not meant to denigrate the progress that Mexico has made since 1910. Her national construction has been considerable. Mexico's accumulation of capital has been great, albeit in the hands of a small segment of the population. Other raw figures show that there are seven times as many roads today as there were in 1940; one-third of all crop land is now irrigated; a rural nation has become a nation in which more than 50% of the population live in towns of twenty thousand of more. The G.N.P./per capita has gone from $150 to $528. Mexico's output increase in the postwar years ranks the country among the first half-dozen countries in the world. Certainly Mexico has outstripped all of her Carribean neighbors except for Cuba and of course, the United States, in the dynamics of her development. An attempt to give a balanced treatment to Mexican development would consider also the horrible conditions of underdevelopment that preceded the revolution.

> Mexico in 1910 ... was a country of poverty, a country in which the vast majority of the people lived in near slavery; in which the standard of living of the wage-earning population was much lower than that of other countries, such as Argentina or Uruguay; a country in which eleven thousand plantation owners had 60 percent of the land; in which 88.4 percent of the agricultural population were *peons*—a condition similar to that of slaves—97 percent were heads of families but landless, and

only 0.02 percent were owners of plantations; in which 13 percent of the population did not speak Spanish; in which 52 percent of the people lived in miserable huts; and in which infant mortality passed the figure of 304 per thousand live births.[7]

From this thumbnail description of poverty, ignorance, and deprivation in Porfirian Mexico through sixty-two years of revolution in which great developmental starts were made, for certain segments of the population (ever-growing in number—Mexico's population should double in thirty years), either little has changed or the focus of deprivation has shifted from a vermin-infested country hut to a rat-infested city slum. In spite of the massive land distribution begun under Cárdenas in the thirties, "over a million heads of rural families remained without land of their own; and with population growth, the number may have risen to nearer two million (out of a total of maybe four million) since 1950."[8]

For 3 million indigenous Indians, the revolution never happened. They "remain economically as badly or maybe worse off than the *poorest* of the forefathers of the time before the Conquest, four and a half centuries ago."[9] In spite of raw development figures, this author saw groups of Indians begging for handouts during Christmas season of 1965 in dazzlingly modern Mexico City.

Mexico's Revolution vs the Socialist Revolutions

Thus it is difficult to balance the Mexican developmental scale. There is always the weight of what has not been done, the knowledge that rapid population growth plus a slow rate of development equal rapid regression and heightened contradictions between rich and poor, developed and underdeveloped, within a nation and between nations. Mexico's developmental quagmire is thrown into particularly sharp relief when one considers the socialist revolutions and their rapid successes in bringing distributive justice to their populations. Mexico's revolution was the first significant social revolution of the twentieth century. It preceded the Soviet upheaval by seven years, the Chinese seizure of power by thirty-nine years, and the Cuban triumph by forty-nine years. Yet today, even the youngest of these three seems to have more effectively established a base for the elimination of social inequity and deprivation than its elderly Mexican predecessor.

This brief but unfavorable comparison between Mexico's eclectic revolution and the socialist revolutions brings into focus what has been one of the major failures of the Mexican revolution. Mexico's revolutionary leaders, although they have prided themselves on their unique path, free of ideological shackles, have never seemed to know in any holistic way where their country was going or should go. This was true of the weak-willed Madero in 1910 and remains true of the present head of what has been called the "Revolutionary Family." The closest Mexico has come to a consistent eschatology is the present panicky and repressive desire to maintain the status quo. This is not to mythologize about the consistency of socialist leaders, like Fidel Castro. Castro has deviated a good deal from his ideal of *Chibasismo,* the pluralistic democracy of the Constitution of 1940, and the liberal humanism of *History Will Absolve Me.* However, there has been an ideological strain which has dominated all of Castro's activity. It is well stated in *History Will Absolve Me:*

> I stated that second consideration on which we based our chances for success was one of social order because we were assured of the *people's* [italics mine] support. When we speak of the people, we do not mean the comfortable ones, the conservative elements of the nation, who welcome any regime of oppression, any dictatorship, any despotism, prostrating themselves before the master of the moment until they grind their foreheads into the ground. When we speak of struggle, the *people* [italics Castro's] means the vast unredeemed masses, to whom all make promises and whom all deceive; we mean the people who yearn for a better, more dignified, and more just nation; who are moved by ancestral aspirations of justice, for they have suffered injustice and mockery, generation after generation; who long for great and wise changes in all aspects of their life; people, who to attain these changes, are ready to give even the very last breath of their lives—when they believe in something or in someone, especially when they believe in themselves.[10]

Castro then proceeds to list the *people* who are to struggle. Here he includes the vast majority of society who have nothing to sell but their labor, and many who have no labor to sell. In this characterization of the people, we hear Fanon's description of decolonization: " 'The last shall be first and the first shall be last.' Decolonization is the putting into practice of this sentence."[11]

Political Development in the 1800s

No such radical understanding of revolutionary necessity has ever directed the Mexican revolution. A study of Mexico's political development from 1810 to the present indicates instead a consistent perversion and co-optation of popular aims in the service of the bourgeoisie. Whereas all Mexicans have been involved in the nation's struggles, the bourgeoisie has consistently triumphed.

The 1810 Rebellion

This bourgeois triumph and popular exclusion can best be understood in its historical progress. A logical place to begin this history is with a *criollo* study group which gathered in Querétaro in 1810. This ostensibly innocuous study group is very interesting, for it contained in kernel the principle contradictions at the center of all later revolutionary struggles in Mexico. This group of *criollos* gathered to study ideas of independence and to build a Creole insurrection against the *gachupines,* the Spaniards who kept the Mexican upper classes from ruling themselves. They wanted nothing more than Mexican autonomy in an alliance with Spain.

These pale demands were for a while drowned in a sea of blood. A Mexican priest, Father Hidalgo y Costillo, who studied with the Querétaro group, unleashed a fantastic rising of the Mexican *campesinos.* This revolt had little to do with either liberalism or self-determination for the affluent few. It concerned land and bread. It did not find its rationalizing ideology in the writings of French and North American intellectuals, but in the syncretized Catholicism of the Virgin of Guadalupe. It is ironic that Hidalgo, co-conspirator of the *criollos,* found himself leading a basic rebellion of Mexico's most wretched. Their rebellion happened by accident and, as a true social upheavel questing for justice, led its leaders until the time that a crucial decision was needed. Padre Hidalgo and the rich landowner Ignacio Allende in one short year of explosive struggle led an army of eighty thousand peasants. Mexico City, the seat of the vice-royalty, defended by only seven thousand loyalist troops, belonged to the people were they but to move against it. The fight up to this point had been spontaneous, anarchic, and very bloody. The Indians and *mestizos* had mercilessly destroyed their *gachupin* and landowning oppressors. Vengeance and death were everywhere in the land. This crimson spectre seemed to be on the priest's mind as he stood before the Spanish stronghold. For at the very moment when a new struggle might have been born, that between the contradictory allies in a victorious misalliance, between the *campesinos* and *criollos,* Father Hidalgo lost his reluctant audacity. Perhaps in fear of an unstoppable popular tide of bloody revolutionary vengeance, perhaps in fear, as Henry Banford Parkes claims, that his anarchic ranks would have been slaughtered by the disciplined Spanish regiments, "he turned his face away from the capital and led his men back to Guanajuato."[12]

Padre Hidalgo's sudden hesitation and perhaps contrition broke the will of his revolutionary army. Thousands of Indians returned to their villages. Most of the *criollos* who had been uneasily allied with the peasant uprising came to terms with the loyalist administration, and the aspirations of Mexico's discontent lay once again under a blanket of Spanish peace.

Hidalgo had started his career as a humane priest, interested in political justice and independence from Spain. When his freedom was in danger because of these ideas, he encouraged an Indian rising. In order to placate the *criollos* and involve them in the struggle, Hidalgo made them officials and officers in his revolutionary army. He told these Creoles that he was struggling to establish an elected congress to govern in the name of the deposed King Ferdinand of Spain. Partly because he was humane and partly because he needed an army of vast numbers, he restored to the Indians their stolen lands and abolished the Indian tribute.

After he was captured, he was said to have reflected on the violence his rebellion had unleashed. The retraction he signed before he was beheaded said that Mexico was not ready for independence, since independence would result only in despotism or anarchy. The religion of aggressive rebellion under the banner of the Virgin of Guadalupe was for many Indians to turn in upon itself for a while and become the faith of the humble, passive, and fatalistic.

Morelos's Revolutionary Efforts

However, the revolutionary aspirations of the people, Indians and Creoles alike, did not perish with Hidalgo. Bands of men, motivated by plunder as well as social justice, swept across Mexico for some years after the death of the rebel priest. The outstanding leader of this post-Hidalgo revolutionary period was another cleric, a parish priest named Jose Maria Morelos. Morelos, whose first commission under Hidalgo gave him command of twenty-five men, in a short while led many thousands. He, like Hidalgo before him, threatened Mexico City. In 1813, within the context of a revolutionary representative assembly, Morelos drafted a revolutionary program. It provided land reform in the break-up of the big *haciendas* and the distribution of small holdings of the peasants. Morelos would have confiscated the property of the rich to share it among the poor and the government. Morelos, although a priest, favored ending the tithe and seizing church lands. He mixed this basic attack on privilege and property with a vision of a democratic republic, "Anáhuac." Anáhuac was to have a parliamentary form of government, elected by universal suffrage and a system of indirect elections. A three-man executive appointed by congress, a supreme court, and a court of *residencia* comprised this liberal body. In addition to planning social and political reform, Morelos executed a plan which dissolved the unity of his command. He came to the congress at Chilpancingo as Generalissimo of the Army. After Chilpancingo, he shared the power to conduct the war with congress. Parkes says that although the congressmen, who were mostly Creole lawyers and priests, were individually capable, they collectively hindered the conduct of the war.

At the same time that the rebel army lost its decisiveness and unity of command, the Spanish General Calleja learned to exploit the contradictions between Indian and Creole to defeat the revolution. The Creoles, fearful of social change, exhausted and threatened by years of war, finally turned to Spain for the most part and supported a royalist militia. By 1816, Morelos was dead. The revolution, begun as a spontaneous response to two distinct forms of oppression against two distinct social groups which never found common ground, ended a year later.

The Alliance that Led to Independence

Thousands had died to crush *gachupin* power and bring agrarian justice to Mexico. However, Mexico's eventual independence from Spain emerged several years later from an alliance of those most threatened by the possibility of agrarian redistribution. The Church, the big *hacendados,* and the liberal Creole bourgeoisie formed an alliance based on their interlocking concerns. The *hacendados* feared the dissatisfied peasant masses; the Church was disturbed about the liberal anticlericalism then emerging from Spain; and the Creole professionals and merchants wanted political power and an end to peasant anarchy and the economic stagnation of Spanish mercantilism. It must be understood that these three groups were by no means separable. The Church was probably Mexico's biggest landowner, and the *hacendado's* son might be a bourgeois lawyer.

Therefore, it was a natural and comfortable group that formed around Iturbide's Plan of Iguala. Agustín de Iturbide had been a repressive, bloody, and venal anti-rebel commander who allied himself with the reactionary Mexican Church. In February of 1820 he set forth a plan for Mexican independence that Parkes claims reiterated the ideas of the original Querétaro conspirators. Its most germane feature, the maintenance of existing property relations, won over all of those in the Mexican upper strata who believed that severance from Spain would further their interests one way or another. For the time being at least, the major class interests of Creole Mexico were protected, and the battle against Spanish domination and peasant rebellion could proceed.

The Church's Role in Mexican History

At this point, it might be instructive to interrupt the historical narrative and notice that one cannot discuss the history of Mexico without continually mentioning the Church and its priests. The clergy were among those most for and most against the struggle of the oppressed. We have already mentioned the leadership roles of Hidalgo and Morelos, the Church as a landowner, and the Church as a faction in the independence movement. At a glance, it would appear that Church and clergy were identifiable threads woven into a secular fabric. But a closer examination of Catholicism in

Mexico reveals a subtler, more pervasive relationship. It may be demonstrated that the entire fabric of Mexican economic, social, and political development have been dyed and processed in the mill of Catholicism.

Contradictions in the Church's Role

It is a mill that has worked in contradictory and paradoxical ways. Much of Mexican history, between the conquest and independence, was made in the name of Christianity. In contrast, the independence movement had anticlerical elements, and the Revolution of 1910 was decidedly anticlerical. The Mexicans themselves are anticlerical, yet they are among the world's most pious, ritualistic people. Catholicism, which was used so successfully to pacify Mexico's Indian people, also set off the violent Indian revolt against the descendents of the conquerors in the nineteenth century. In periods of despair, religion made things tolerable by providing hope and reinforcing fatalism. It licensed the hierarchy and cruelty that were necessary to maintain the inequities of each of the successive social systems. It suggested martyrdom rather than practical action as a solution to injustice, and encouraged exorcistic violence against the rich which alternated with periods of helpless passivity.

The answer to these contradictions lies in the complexity of the Mexican class hierarchy and the historical process that both class and religion have been subjected to. When Hernán de Cortes, seething under frustrated ambition in Cuba, landed in Yucatan, he pacified both his own unruly crew and the Indians who confronted him with the cross of Catholicism. This, the Catholicism of Spain, was capable of an extremely complex mission. It was the Catholicism of conquest and vengeance. It arrived in the New World fresh from the destruction of Moorish power in Iberia. It was a religion whose triumph depended on its ability to motivate tne rationalize violence. It was a faith conditioned by its medieval function of easing misery and death. It explained why human life was the least stable element in the medieval landscape. It offered the eternal to minds too conscious of mortality. It supplied the myth that was a substitute for comprehension in an insecure and incomprehensible world. And, as an accomplice to the prevailing political power, it justified the fact that the rich ruled and the poor suffered but submitted.

The Church and the Conquerors

Catholicism was to be as serviceable in New Spain. It gave the conquerors unity, discipline, courage, and most of all, justification. They conquered not only for plunder, but for the glory of God. They conquered heathens and shepherded thousands into the fold of Christianity.

The Spaniards used their religion to continue the lessons of hierarchy and exploitation that the Indian religions had taught before. The religion of the Aztecs had conveniently predicted the coming of the Spaniards. There existed in pre-Columbian lore a white god who would one day come from the east to claim the Indian world as his own. His name was Quetzalcoatl. When Cortés arrived with arms and horses—loud and magical weapons and enormous supernatural animals that men could ride—the Indians believed he was an emissary of Quetzalcoatl. Cortés did not fail to capitalize on this confusion. One of his first acts was to smash the Indian idols and replace them with Christian symbols. This is not to say that the whole indigenous population was instantly converted or convinced that religion and submission to the Spanish were eternal correlates. Although Cortés seemed successful in controlling Montezuma and the Aztec city of Tenochtitlán for six months, the slaughter of the Spanish force on June 30, 1520, testifies to the very imperfect control exercised by the Spaniards and their aggressive Catholicism. The conquest and slaughter were followed by reconquest, all of which illustrates a contradiction in the religion and purpose of the Spaniards. Catholicism was intended to pacify the Indians, but it was offered to them on the blade of a sword. Thus, it was a faith of submission, not one of peace. In fact, Spanish Catholicism coincided neatly with the subservience and violence that characterized Indian culture before the conquest, and perhaps it succeeded in Mexico because it contradicted so little and licensed so much. (For instance, the Mexican bandits in Traven's celebrated novel, *The Treasure of Sierra Madre,* wore religious medals for protection.)

It would be inexact to think that the religion of the conquerors ever became the religion of the conquered. The struggles of the *campesinos* under Hidalgo, Morelos, Guerrero, and Matamoros against the *gachupines* can be viewed as a religious war. Hidalgo carried the Virgin of Guadalupe into battle, while the Spanish viceroy, besieged in the capital, prayed to the Virgin of the Remedies. The Virgin of Guadalupe is symbolic of the religion of the oppressed. She is a syncretized Indian-Catholic deity whose existence confirmed for both Indian and *gachupin* their inherent differences. This inherency reifies the differences between classes. It justifies and rationalizes the practices of the upper classes, for it gives a transcendental basis for class.

Religion was a first as well as final element obscuring the real reasons for and methods of dealing with the antagonisms which grew out of the relationships between the social strata of Mexican society. Indians could be worked, slain, and enslaved not only because they were Indians, but also because their Catholic variant was a function and affirmation of that difference and thus a license to European exploitation. Indians could be protected from total annihilation through inhuman labor, not because they were human, but because they were Christian.

When Indians and *mestizos* rose up, it was the spiritual world and not just their objective conditions of servitude and oppression that justified the rebellion. The battle was fought on the ground, but its mercilessness and carnage were permitted because the men engaged in the battle were vehicles of transcendental Catholic justice.

The Myth of Two Cultures

The existence of two Catholic traditions strengthened the myth of two cultures, which is perpetuated by such distinguished scholars as Oliver La Farge and Oscar Lewis. One culture is that of the upper strata, which is relatively modern and western. The modernity of this group justifies their social rank and economic leadership. The other culture is that of the vast majority—Indians and *mestizos* who live in poverty and practice an Indianized Catholicism retaining the superstitions of the past. If their lives are unsatisfactory, the myth contends that it is because their cultural patterns are disintegrating under the onslaught of Western technology. This latter culture Lewis calls the "culture of poverty."

Using these concepts of one country—two cultures, the rich accept class differences and therefore rationalize away exploitation. Similarly, the poor capitulate or rebel, doing both in a syndrome which suggests Frantz Fanon's theory of "avoidance."

> It is as if plunging into a fraternal bloodbath allowed them to ignore the obstacle, and to put off till later the choice, nevertheless inevitable, which opens up the question of armed resistance to colonialism. Thus collective autodestruction in a very concrete form is one of the ways in which the native's muscular tension is set free. All these patterns of conduct are those of the death reflex when faced with danger, a suicidal behavior which proves to the settler (whose existence and domination is by them all the more justified) that these men are not reasonable human beings. In the same way the native manages to by-pass the settler. A belief in fatality removes all blame from the oppressor; the cause of misfortunes and of poverty is attributed to God; He is Fate. In this way the individual accepts the disintegration ordained by God, bows down before the settler and his lot, and by a kind of interior restabilization, acquires a stony calm.[13]

Much of this applies to Mexico. The poor and exploited fatalistically accept their condition or strike out at each other. But Mexico is different in that the violence occasionally leaves the *cantinas* and *barrios* of the poor and turns against the oppressors. At this point, religion steps in and both blesses the revolt and obscures its causes, so that a few *hacendados* are killed, but the system of exploitation survives.

Later, in a discussion of *Zapatismo,* I shall explore more fully how this Mexican "world outlook," confirmed in its two Catholicisms, prevented the agrarian rebels from seeing Mexico as it is: one society, not two, wherein distinctive cultural outlooks obscure vicious exploitation. The two-culture theorists explain the brutalization of poverty as a product of a land tenure system or the "onslaught of the Age of Technology," ignoring the totalitarian nature of the system of exploitation. In these semi-analyses, the accumulation of wealth and power in the hands of an increasingly smaller number of people is not mentioned as the first concommitant of poverty for the greater number. Nor is the subjugation of Mexico's labor and commodity market to a world market, whose decision-making center is elsewhere, ever credited with exacerbating poverty and the dehumanizing aspects of its "culture."

Anticlericalism as a Revolutionary Theme

Mexico's Church, by its use and abuse of power, by accumulation of enormous land, wealth, and power, continually throughout Mexico's history, moved further and further away from the mass of the population. Because of this, the Church hierarchy and many of its priests lived lives which were the very antithesis of the humility and passivity they encouraged among the population. While they preached spiritual redemption, they sought temporal power. While they emphasized spirituality and purity, and in some cases presided over the mortification of the flesh in rituals of flagellation, they indulged themselves with concubines. It is not surprising that in all the rebellions that have racked Mexico, anticlericalism was a great theme. Latins have always been able to distinguish the value of spirituality from the corruption and irrelevance of the Church.

The constitutions of 1857 and of 1917 both limit the Church's many past privileges. In the period from 1926 to 1929 there was a virtual war between President Calles and the Church.* This was not a war of propaganda, but of bullets and dynamite. When Calles enforced the anticlerical clauses of the constitution, which had been ignored to this point, some middle-class groups along with some of the peasantry rushed to the aid of the Church. They formed guerrilla bands known as *cristeros.* They burned government schools, shot government officials, and attained a high point of violent rebellion in April 1927 when they dynamited the Mexico-Guadalajara train, killing a hundred passengers in the explosion and fire. Calles' actions and popular disgust with the *cristeros* finally broke the might of the Mexican Church. This violent period provided a number of "revolutionary" generals the opportunity to plunder the wealth of the states in which the rebellion took place. These "anti-Catholic" military chieftains robbed and shot wealthy Catholics and lined their own pockets. They drove many of these Catholics unwillingly into the ranks of the *cristeros.* In this way, they prolonged and magnified the rebellion. This larger rebellion provided the

*Calles' term of office ended in 1928, but he continued to control the government for several years after.

military with further excuses to rob everyone in the warring areas. A General
Ferreira herded sixty thousand peasants into concentration camps in northern Jalisco, while his army raked the wealth of the land into its own coffers
and burned what could not be plundered.

The Church Today

Mexico is now at peace with the Church. Although the power of the church
is no longer as pervasive as it was, relatively speaking Mexico has one of the
largest churches in the Americas. According to a recent Rand study, Mexico
is second only to Brazil in the number of religious personnel doing service
there: 33,648 priests, brothers, and nuns were active in Mexico in 1968. This
is almost 8,000 more religious personnel than are working in Colombia.
Mexico is again second only to Brazil in number of parishes, monasteries,
and convents. Although Mexico is far from first in the number of Catholic
school students as a percentage of all students above the primary level,
45.8% of this category of students attend Catholic schools. Altogether, as
of 1968, 587,000 Mexican students attended Catholic schools. Mexico also
seems to be replacing its retiring and dying priests at a rate above that
sufficient to maintain the number of active priests at its present level.[14]
These figures remind us that the church is able to sustain its role as a major
value implanter, as a confirmational element in the myth of the two cultures,
and as a vehicle for "avoidance."

At the conclusion of the chapter, I will discuss the corporate solution to
Mexico's antagonistic contradictions. It is ironic that the governing formula
of the avowedly anticlerical revolutionary government should in some ways
reflect a medieval Catholic concept of the proper form of government.

Political Development
in the Early 1900s

Revolution of 1910

The Revolution of 1910, in its inception, its struggles, and its increasingly
unstable institutional form, has reflected the perpetuation of narrow class
interests and always the lack of an holistic analysis of Mexican society. That
the anatagonisms between a largely landless peasantry and a small class of
wealthy landholders, bankers, and industrialists were not to be solved by the
1910 overthrow of Diaz can best be seen in the programs, perspectives, and
practices of the leading protagonists of the revolution.

Francisco I. Madero was the son of a wealthy landholding family in the
northern state of Coahula. He was thirty-eight years old in 1911 and well
in the tradition of Mexican liberalism when he assumed the presidency soon

after Porfirio Diaz resigned. Diaz had ruled the country for thirty years. He practiced what he claimed was the most modern scientific method of government. Since he was a positivist and above politics, he allowed no politics in Mexico. He wanted no challenges as he systematically sold Mexico's resources and labor to North American and European capitalists. Diaz controlled rebellion among the peasants by organizing what were called *los rurales,* a rural police force consisting of bandits. The bandits were permitted to practice their trade of plunder within the system to protect the system. The conditions in which thirty years of Porfirian rule had left the country were summarized early in this chapter.

Madero conceived of his assumption of power as a revolution. He offered Mexico's suffering millions a new brand of political science. Its major feature was the phrase, "effective suffrage, no reelections." In 1910, Madero offered the people his Plan of San Luis Potosí, a plan to replace tyranny with a democratic form of government. In that Madero felt that violence might be necessary to overthrow the Porfirian tyranny, his plan designated certain rules of revolutionary warfare—prohibiting, for example, the use of expanding bullets and the shooting of prisoners. In this plan, Madero placed his credentials for leadership before the Mexican people.

"I have very well realized that, if the people have designated me as their candidate for the presidency, it is not because they have had an opportunity to discover in me the qualities of a statesman or of a ruler, but the virility of the patriot determined to sacrifice himself, if need be, to obtain liberty and to help the people free themselves from the odious tyranny that oppresses them."[15] Among the details of the plan for a new government—free elections, rules of war, and Madero's credentials—there is astonishingly little mention of social and economic reform. The problem of agrarian reform is dealt with in one vague, well-intentioned paragraph.

> In abuse of the law on public lands numerous proprietors of small holdings, in their greater part Indians, have been dispossessed of their lands by rulings of the department of public development (*fomento*) or by decisions of the tribunals of the Republic. As it is just to restore to their former owners the lands of which they were dispossessed in such an arbitrary manner, such rulings and decisions are declared subject to revision, and those who have acquired them in such an immoral manner, or their heirs, will be required to restore them to their former owners, to whom they shall also pay an indemnity for the damages suffered. Solely in case those lands have passed to third persons before the promulgation of this plan shall the former owners receive an indemnity from those in whose favor the dispossession was made.[16]

Except for a few words about the waste, degradation, and misery which the scientific oligarchy were causing, this is all that Madero offers on the social and economic conditions of his nation. One is predisposed to believe in

Madero's sincerity—he risked too much to be an opportunist. He firmly trusted that Mexico would cure its ills through political reform. Universal suffrage, peaceful succession, no reelection, and checks and balances were at the center of his desires for Mexico. He lived his life to the very end as an aristocrat. Vasconcelos tells of his last lunch with Madero, when the besieged president was an unofficial prisoner in the hands of the counter-revolutionary officers. "In the dining room of the palace we sat down to a light but tastefully prepared meal. A Barsac wine, drawn from the old stocks, gave the glasses a golden greenish glow."[17]

Madero's contact with the people and their poverty was that of a benevolent prince among his subjects. Vasconcelos writes of Madero's last attempt to appeal to the people, while he was Huerta's prisoner in the presidential palace and after a palace confrontation with his captors in which people on both sides were killed:

> As soon as the corpses had been removed, Madero gathered his few followers and strode to the balcony of the palace, intending to call on the people to aid him. Outside the streets were totally deserted, showing the care Huerta had taken to isolate the prisoner. In any case, the people would not move. A few days earlier, after printing a proclamation calling on them to defend the government, we had driven in a car through all the humble wards where once we had strong support. Everywhere the people received us with distrust. And they were right, for we did not give them arms; the city was no longer ours.[18]

His total failure of analysis was a failure of naivete, a naivete conditioned by his lack of contact with and trust in the people. The real significance of Madero, and of his revolution, was that in the downfall of the "scientific oligarchy," the liberal bourgeoisie, stifled for years by repression, by their own greed in the face of foreign capital, for thirty years now almost had the political power to run the country for their unlimited benefit. However, before they could institutionalize that power, they had to deal with the newly unleashed contradiction contained in the claims of Mexico's landless poor.

Zapata

As Madero's view was naive, Zapata's was narrow. After the long, nearly victorious struggle of the Revolution of 1910, its leader was dead, its ideology co-opted, and its demands only partially fulfilled. Emiliano Zapata, unlike Madero, was a man of the people. Womack tells how the people in Zapata's village thought of him.

> If he dandied up on holidays and trotted around the village and into the nearby town of Villa de Ayala on a silver-saddled horse, the people never questioned that he was still one of them. Despite his fine horses

and suits, Anenecuilcans never referred to him as Don Emiliano, which would have removed him from the guts and flies and manure and mud of local life, sterilizing the real respect they felt for him into a squire's vague respectability. He was one of their own, they felt in Anenecuilco, and it never made them uncomfortable to treat him so. 'Miliano, they called him, and when he died, *pobrecito,* poor little thing. To them he was a neighbor, a younger cousin who could lead the clan, a beloved nephew as rough and true as seasoned timber.[19]

The revolution in which Zapata led the *campesinos* of Morelos released great energies in Mexico. For Madero, the revolution meant political reform. For the liberal Creole bourgeoisie who surrounded him, it meant power and the opportunity for the dynamic development and exploitation of a stagnant, imperialist-dominated economy. But for Zapata and the *campesinos,* the revolution promised a return to the Indian communal land system, which in an agrarian void might have had dynamic possibilities. These *campesinos* hoped that the revolution would break the back of 400 years of *gachupin* and *hacendado* control of the land. Recall the land tenure figures quoted earlier in this chapter. "Mexico in 1910 . . . [was] a country in which eleven thousand plantation owners had 60 percent of the land; in which 88.4 percent of the agricultural population were peons . . . 97 percent were heads of families but landless, and only 0.02 percent were owners of plantations."[20]

The revolutionary Creoles also wanted to oust the old *hacendados* because they saw great business opportunity in these lands. What havoc this might have brought to the *pueblos* in the displacement of population and the thwarting of *pueblo* autonomy was not crucial to these newly unrestrained business revolutionaries. But the *campesinos* wanted the land for themselves and the *pueblos.* This idea was the major thrust of *Zapatismo.* In that Madero and the revolutionary generals who followed him into the presidency neglected this claim on the land, Zapata and his *companeros* fought, burned, and punished the middle-class revolutionaries from Mexico City. The heart of *Zapatismo* is contained in the Plan of Ayala, first proclaimed in November 1911. The Plan called Madero "inept at realizing the promises of the revolution of which he was the author, because he has betrayed the principles with which he tricked the will of the people and was able to get into power; incapable of governing, because he has no respect for the law and justice of the *pueblos,* and a traitor to the fatherland because he is humiliating in blood and fire Mexicans who want liberties so as to please the *científicos,* landlords, and bosses who enslave us."[21]

The Zapatistas go on to state, "From today on we begin to continue the revolution begun by him [Madero] until we achieve the overthrow of the dictatorial powers which exist."[22] The Zapatistas base their continuity with Madero's revolution on the paragraph in the Plan of San Luis Potosí which deals with the restoration of land stolen from the *pueblos*. The Morelos revolutionaries define their additions to Madero's promise, especially in Articles 6 and 7 of the Plan of Ayala.

> 6. As an additional part of the plan we invoke, we give notice, that [regarding] the fields, timber, and water which the landlords, científicos, or bosses, have usurped, the pueblos or citizens who have the titles corresponding to those properties will immediately enter into possession of that real estate of which they have been despoiled by the bad faith of our oppressors, maintaining at any cost with arms in hand the mentioned possession and the usurpers who consider themselves with a right to them [those properties] will deduce it before the special tribunals which will be established on the triumph of the revolution.

> 7. In virtue of the fact that the immense majority of Mexican pueblos and citizens are owners of no more than the land they walk on, suffering the horrors of poverty without being able to improve their social condition in any way or to dedicate themselves to Industry or Agriculture, because lands, timber, and water are monopolized in a few hands, for this cause there will be expropriated the third part of those monopolies from the powerful proprietors of them, with prior indemnization, in order that the pueblos and citizens of Mexico may obtain ejidos, colonies, and foundations for pueblos, or fields for sowing or laboring, and the Mexicans' lack of prosperity and well-being may improve in all and for all.[23]

This plan remained an accurate reflection of Zapata's analysis of Mexico's woes and their remedies throughout the struggle. Womack uses interesting terms to describe the feelings of the Zapatista's about the plan. "The Zapatistas swore by their Plan de Ayala. . . . The Zapatista chiefs considered the plan a veritable catholicon, much more than a program of action, almost a Scripture."[24]

This unwavering reverence for a plan drafted at the very beginning of a long struggle would appear static and reactionary to the modern revolutionary, schooled in dialectics, who perceives that everything is changing all the time. Castro's *History Will Absolve Me* was a tactical device, mostly reconsidered and evolved through years of struggle. In a sense, *Zapatismo* was more Catholic than the Church in its reverence for fixed absolutes. This is not to denigrate the plan itself, for its power to gain such loyalty indicates what an accurate reflection it was of the feelings and aspirations of the people who died for it. It must also be stated that although there was a gap of a decade and a half between the time that Zapata's chiefs reconciled themselves with the revolutionary government and the time of Cárdenas' agrarian reform, the ideas of the Plan of Ayala were translated into Cárdenas' agrarian experiment. However, the shortcomings and limited nature of the current agrarian program and the failure of Mexico to achieve distributive or participatory justice after sixty years of revolution are in some way related to the fact that the agrarian revolutionaries never transcended their almost totally agrarian analysis. The bourgeoisie who siezed power never failed to see how capital gained in land and realty speculation or earned by controlling price and distribution of crops could be integrated with industrial and finance capital for the further accumulation and investment of capital. Zapata was at the beginning and the end of his struggle an agrarian humanist. He was concerned with land and the people who lived and worked on it. The people he struggled against placed a different, less human, but economically more comprehensive value on the land.

The Problems of Stability

Class Differences and Instability

Although Mexico in 1910 was a basically agrarian country, whose population was mostly rural, its potential as something more had of course been recognized as early as 1519. However, in 1910 as in 1519, those who profited most from Mexico's raw material potential were not Mexican. Intensified imperialism, which busily constructed an infrastructure of roads, ports, and railroads to serve the dynamic exploitation of Mexico's wealth during the thirty years of the Porfiriato, was a key factor in the Revolution of 1910. The administrative and legal talents of the bourgeoisie had been exploited by foreign business along with the country's raw materials, and now that same bourgeoisie saw their chance to benefit directly from Mexico's wealth. While Zapata wanted land in a basically agrarian country, the bourgeoisie wanted everything in a potentially industrial country. In a very profound sense, Zapata's dreams were conservative, while his enemies, socially and politically conservative, were economically dynamic.

Today Mexico is more urban that rural. Between 1950 and 1960, towns and cities having a population over 20,000 inhabitants have grown by 16,-135,000 people form 11,265,000 to 27,300,000 respectively. In the same time period the rural population increased by only 5,430,000 from 15,-170,000 inhabiting farms and rural villages in 1950 to 20,500,000 in 1970. Given that the total population increase in that twenty-year period was 21,375,000, from 26,435,000 to 47,800,000 one can see the phenomenal growth of the urban sector. From a demographic point alone, Mexico of 1970 was a radically different country from the one that saw Madero triumph and die and Zapata struggle valiantly on horseback against landowners, *científicos,* and bosses. The contradictions that wracked Mexico through the nineteenth century and early twentieth century have been modified, complicated, and in certain ways intensified. Mexico has changed and her world context has changed. President Calles, to a small degree, and Cardenas much more broadly, instituted land reform. The *ejido* system, based on ancient Aztec and Spanish landholding principles (wherein title to the land is held by a rural village, organized as a communal group), is a major method of dealing with land tenure under the agrarian reform. Some land, especially in the north where the communal tradition was not strong, was distributed as small holdings. While much of the land remains organized as large holdings, workers on some *haciendas* have been given small subsistence plots to supplement their wages. An *ejido* credit bank has been established to answer the need for credit at reasonable rates. However, corruption, inefficiency, bureaucratism, powerful economic-political interests, and consequent lack of ability, consciousness, and incentive among many *campesinos* have all worked to undermine the system. The rural aspect of the contradiction thus remains unresolved, but evolved and therefore different.

Mexico's population in 1910 was 90% lower class. Of this 90%, the great majority were *campesinos.* However, since the 1940s, Mexico's emphasis on industrialization has increased the number of non-agricultural workers in the lower class and has reduced the proportion of people in what is now called the "popular" class. It is difficult to determine what the boundaries of this current popular class are, but to be sure, the industrial and service workers and lumpen urban dwellers comprise a larger proportion of this class than they did in 1910.

Instability and rebellion before the revolution and during its first decade resulted from contradictions among a ruling class, a politically unenfranchised middle group, and the *campesinos.* Today the field of potential and actual struggle is complicated by the diversification of the popular sector as well as the enlargement of the middle group. A reliable informant reports that during the 1968 "student" riots, revolutionary cadre were able to organize committees among all economic sectors of the popular class. The complexities of the lower class, expressed in the differences among industrial workers, *ejiditarios,* small holders, landless rural people, lumpen urban dwellers, and indigenous Indians, make the job of social analysis more difficult but do not override the fact that the revolution never did resolve the extreme tensions between the popular class and its rulers. These tensions seem to be worsening. Although Howard Cline says that social mobility has increased the middle sector by recruiting from the popular class, 50% of the population "live at a level substantially below the minimum, both economic and socially."[25] Mexico's great population growth, partly due to improved medical facilities, and the general third-world climate of revolutionary anti-imperialism should exacerbate these tensions in the future.

The Management of Conflict

Given these unresolved but increasingly complex tensions, one of the most interesting features of the revolution is the skillful way in which the revolutionary leadership has managed conflict in the society. In effect, the major achievement of the revolution has been its ability, after a long struggle, to maintain enough stability so that significant development could take place. The key to Mexican stability is the ruling formula of the *Partido Revolutionary Institucional.* This formula has a number of major facets. Two of these, institutionalized authoritism and the corporate structure of the party, are perfectly consistent with Mexico's Catholic culture, whose values and mechanisms worked to rationalize and obfuscate extremely sharp social contradictions during 300 years of Spanish rule.[26] These culturally available mechanisms will be discussed in some detail below. They form a context in which the usual systemic methods have been sufficient for stability in the past. In that the P.R.I. has established itself as the primary power broker in society, the party is in a position to co-opt potential dissidents. As we shall see below, the party's organization and membership is broad enough and intensive enough to encourage and include leaders from all sectors of society. The P.R.I. has the power, money, positions, and patronage to distribute. There has also been a modicum of social mobility (adroitly exaggerated by public relations) and so many tempting gradations between life at the luxurious, powerful top and the wretched, multitudinous bottom that potential dissenters channel their aggressiveness into the mobility scramble. Interestingly, the myth of mobility, a major theme of political propaganda, is sufficiently strong to make many of those who "don't make it" feel unworthy and therefore apathetic. The cost to society is crime rather than direct political challenge.

Institutionalized corruption also takes pressure off the system. The sale of favors and dispensations gives even the oppressed some feeling that the system is manipulable. It also takes pressure off the government to pay its civil servants better by making the lowest-ranking bureaucrat into an entrepreneur. However, as with most mechanisms of control, corruption has its contradictions for the system. The Church had already learned this in Mexico.

Andre Gunder Frank points out that the government subsidizes corn and movies in Mexico City—its bread and circuses for the poor. Mexico City itself, as the primary recipient of internal immigrants, has up to the present been a pressure valve. Given Mexico's population boom and the country's continued agrarian problems, the *Distrito Federal* has a limited future in this capacity.

When all else fails, there is always repression. The severity of repression in Mexico reflects a history and a culture in which violence has been a central theme, a characteristic of societies whose masses are poverty-stricken and oppressed. If Mexico appears especially so, the reader should consider the contemporary history of South Asian, African, and Middle Eastern nations, to say nothing of Latin American neighbors such as Colombia, Guatemala, and Haiti. The best analysis of the mass psychology of political violence is Frantz Fanon's. Violence is institutionalized among oppressed people by the soldiers and police of the dominant group because domination cannot be achieved by the subtler, more harmonious means used to exploit workers in advanced countries. The policeman or the soldier "is the bringer of violence into the home and into the mind of the native."[27]

Violence as a Part of Mexican Life

In the context of this fact of life, Mexico, from the conquest through the present, with some lapses in the 1940s and 1950s, has chronicled a bloody enough tale. Madero, Zapata, and Villa were all slain martyrs of different concepts of the revolution. To take power was to take power away and to expect to be challenged. Madero, in the Plan of San Luis Potosí, planned and called for violence. In the novels of Fuentes and in the accounts of Mexico given by Traven one reads of the spectre of death that has gripped Mexico. In this there is cultural continuity with the pre-Cortesian religion of the Indians. A daily gift of life was given in supplication to the gods to still their deadly potential. Institutional violence—unbearable overwork, disease, malnutrition—was the fate of subjugated Indians who worked the mines. The situation was not improved hundreds of years later during the *Porfiriato,* when for thirty years 90% of the population suffered similar indirect violence. It was the *rurales* of Diaz who practiced the *ley fuga* (the shooting of prisoners) with rebels and criminals alike in order to maintain stability for the old dictator.

Violence, death, and martyrdom are reflected in the iconography of the Mexican country churches. Wooden figures of Christ are colorful, dripping blood from the Sacred Heart and down from the Crown of Thorns. Central to Mexican Catholicism are the Virgins of Guadalupe and of Papoan, symbols of the martyred woman who suffers and gives up her sons to death. It is revealing to listen to a Mexican sermon on the glories of suffering and the rewards of martyrdom. In that the religion centralizes death, it rationalizes death's omnipresence. Catholicism thus captured and glorified the central theme of successive oppressive societies in Mexico.

Machismo, fatalism, and martyrdom are three characteristic Mexican ways of dealing with an oppressive life. *Machismo* means more than masculinity because it implies living up to all challenges in defiance of the continuous challenge of death. It is a human affirmation to steal life in the face of oppression. Martyrdom is the reward given to someone who loses his life in defense of the *machismo* and *dignidad* of his people. Fatalism ties the triad together. A man will die in defense of his *machismo, si Diós quiera.* And if God wills life, one will not be a dead hero but a live one.

In this context of ever-present violent challenge, one expects a violent response. To have political power is to have an augmented *machismo* to defend. Both the challenger and the challenged seem to have understood the violent implications of the struggle for political power. Given this history of violence, the continuance of institutional violence for the still too many poor, and the cultural supports of violence (both religious and psychological in Mexico), it is not surprising to hear ever-expanded tales of bloody repression in today's Mexico. It is difficult to get an accurate estimate of the number of demonstrators slaughtered in the extended riots of 1968. The summer of 1971 brought new rebellion in Mexico City and again heavy-handed response from the government. Reports from student participants in the Mexico City risings about increasing numbers of urban and rural guerrilla groups would lead one to expect an intensification of challenge and repression throughout the decade.

Recent Political Leadership

Obregón and Calles

All of the available techniques for maintaining stability cannot be separated from the ability of the government to practice them. A government that is weak for other reasons would not survive its first skirmish; the ability to manipulate is an exercise of power, not its base, just as investment is the further use of money one has already made. The Mexican ruling group consolidated its power first through the personal strength and personality of Alvaro Obregón. Obregón was in effect a *caudillo*. His personality elicited grudging allegiance from the agrarian rebels and confidence from a bourgeois class seeking stability after the ineptitude of Carranza. Moreno has said of Obregón, "His caudillistic personality elicited allegiance and his political instincts led to the elimination of competing potential *caudillos* and enemies."[28] Obregón's caudillismo brought enough stability to Mexico so that another *caudillo,* Plutarco Elías Calles, was able to begin the job of institutionalizing power. His retirement from office in 1928 at the end of his legal term disinterred Madero's revolutionary cry, "No reelections." Thus Calles added revolutionary legitimacy to caudillistic strength. His programs of road building, health and sanitation campaigns, and irrigation projects gave to his regime the fleshed-out legitimacy of revolutionary dynamism. Calles also strengthened his claim to leadership and gave reality to the revolutionary significance of his regime by attacking Mexico's revolutionary pariahs, the Church and North American business interests. The *cristero* rebellion was smashed, most of the Church's perquisites were abolished. In order to continue to rule from behind the scenes, Calles founded the *Partido Nacional Revolucionario.* It grouped contradictory elements and leaders, distributed some power to all of them, and then maintained Calles's rule and stability in a potentially violent country.

Cárdenas

After two fairly subservient presidents had fronted for Calles's growing conservatism and corruption, Lazaro Cárdenas was tapped by the former president, his first mistake in the choice of a front man. Cárdenas, who had appeared to be a dependable ally, turned out to be his own man. But ironically, his principled rejection of Calles and his politics did more for the interest of Calles's big business supporters than Calles himself was able to do. Cárdenas's charisma, socialistic programs, and above all, his establishment of a corporate formula for Mexican rule dealt a *coup de gras* to political instability in Mexico. Cárdenas institutionalized power and was able to develop the manipulative techniques for the maintenance of power that we have already referred to. The salient result of all this was that the bourgeoisie were in a position to dominate the development of the country.

After Calles's conservatism helped business re-entrench itself in the economy, Cárdenas seemed to march off in another economic and social direction. His program and his rhetoric were socialistic. He encouraged the organization both of labor and the agrarian sector. By overseeing the foundation of the *Confederacion de Trabajadores de Mexico* (C.T.M.) and the *Confederacion Nacional Campesina* (C.N.C.) he captured and incorporated the revolutionary energy and leadership of the popular classes into what were to be the established political channels. In that Cárdenas supported labor strikes and greatly accelerated land distribution, popular leaders trusted his organizational sponsorship. Cárdenas expanded the government's educational effort. Through his education reforms, he attempted to incorporate all elements, even the Indians, into the Mexican nation.

Cárdenas, like Obregón and Calles before him, was a strong man with great personal magnetism. He attracted great loyalty. His neutralization of Calles and the sweep of his programs were integral to his personal strength. During his presidency his power was final and absolute. In that his power was used within the legitimate context and aspirations of Mexico, his rule seemed to strengthen almost all sectors without exacerbating antagonisms, and could be characterized as authoritistic. Cárdenas was thus more than a *caudillo.* He was the strong man who tightened legitimate order. He was in a historical line of succession from the legitimate Spanish monarchy and among the king-presidents who from time to time have emerged in Latin America. This facet of Cárdenas's rule was thus very much in continuity with Mexico's Spanish-Catholic legacy. It echoes Thomas's characterization of the prince as a strong moderator. Another extremely important facet of Cárdenas's rule was the governing formula he established.

Cárdenas' "Socialism"

It was mentioned above that Cárdenas's program was socialistic. He emphasized the lower classes in his programs. School books during the Cárdenas period glorified labor, the worker, and the class struggle.[29]

One would think that Cárdenas saw socialism as Mexico's future. When Cárdenas took Calle's loosely constructed P.N.R. and reshaped it into the corporate *Partido Revolucionario Mexicano* (P.R.M.), the popular sectors of labor and agriculture constituted half of the party's sectors.

However, this great organizational effort did not result in the evolution of socialism. Mexican social and political stability were to be achieved within the context of *corporatism,* a political plan born out of sharply hierarchical medieval Catholic Europe and popularized by contemporary Italian and Spanish Fascism.

Corporatism is a formula for the creation of a unified social order out of the "natural" diversity within society. It must be remembered that Mexico's diversity has resulted in violent bloody anarchy throughout the nineteenth century. It was only the stern rule of Diaz which placed a lid on this disorder. The Revolution of 1910 was an expression of the ever-intensifying class and personal contradictions in Mexican society. The revolution did not immediately replace the authority it destroyed. Anarchy reemerged, but the revolution derived a formula for order within which Mexico could be modernized. Cárdenas, although paying lip service to Mexico's workers and peasants, de-emphasized the class struggle and "resolved" the conflict with the elevation of the working class within the idea of a state of class cooperation. The revolution itself, embodied in a party, appeared to replace any particular class as the leader of the nation. And one man, the leader of the party and possibly the president of the nation, would be the ultimate ruler of the new ordering of Mexican diversity. Cárdenas's rule and his ruling formula recall the elements of St. Thomas' prescriptions for the organization of society. There is an ordering of diversity into a peaceful unity. St. Thomas believed that "one can more efficaciously bring about unity than a group of several ... therefore the rule of one man is more useful than the rule of many."

However, just as Thomas recognized the merits of a mixed form of government containing elements of monarchy, aristocracy, and democracy, the Cárdenas formula allows for the rule of the leader tempered by a party of popular participation and an aristocratic inner circle, what Bradenburg calls the "revolutionary family."

The party thus created the myth of the great partnership. It appeared that workers, *campesinos,* and the bourgeoisie were in a self-conscious partnership to create progress for all through modernization. That infrastructural changes have taken place cannot be denied. Some of them have been cited earlier in the chapter. However, neither Cárdenas nor the P.R.M. or P.R.I., as it is now called, ever destroyed Mexican class hierarchy. It may be that the upper classes have some new incumbents, but this strengthens rather than destroys the class system. Thus the "partnership" has been very unequal. One sector of today's P.R.I. dominates. As the middle class dominates Mexico economically, the C.N.O.P. (*Confederacion Nacional de Organizaciones Populares*) or middle-class sector of the party dominates politically. Its members have money, influence, education, and international ties. In this corporate party, in which workers, peasants, and bourgeoisie are supposed to discover cooperative fulfillment, the bourgeoisie sets policy while the legitimate demands of the working class and peasants are diverted by co-opted popular class leadership. Apart from a certain labor aristocracy, the major segments of labor and the peasantry stagnate in this co-opted and antagonistic bind within the structure of the party.

This co-optation goes beyond P.R.I. labor and peasant leadership. Although the P.R.I. is Mexico's only really effective party, other parties do exist and pretend to contend. Sometimes and on a very limited local level, an organization such as the *Partido Accion Nacional* is allowed to win an election. This "competition" is not only permitted by the P.R.I. but often underwritten by the party. In the 200-seat national legislature, 25 seats are respectfully reserved for the opposition. This does more than pay lip service to diversity. Allowing the so-called opposition to exist and to criticize within the system is certainly a safety valve and an additional vehicle for co-optation. In an article entitled "Control and Co-optation in Mexican Politics," Bo Anderson and James D. Cockroft describe the evolution of the twin techniques of co-optation and repression.

> The coöptation principle reflects . . . a very basic concern that goes back to the times right after the revolutionary wars: the need to "nationalize" politics in the country. After the wars politics in Mexico was very fragmented. Local bosses . . . controlled many areas of the country, maintained their own armies or bands of strongmen, and often acted independently of or in defiance of the national authorities. . . . The party that began to be built in the 1920's had as one of its tasks to overcome this fragmentation, to build an organization which although ideally sensitive to local needs and demands, could be an instrument in the construction of a modern, rather centralized state and the maintenance of social peace. . . . The party chose to be ideologically pragmatic and vague, in order to accommodate the various groups. Groups of different persuasion were offered rewards and concessions in return for loyalty to the party and the regime. It was also, however, made very clear that the party would not tolerate any strong centers of power that were outside of the party or not allied with the party. If coöptation failed strong-arm methods were used. Many of the local caudillos and caciques were assassinated, on orders from the regime. Gradually there emerged the pattern we have seen: the PRI attempts to coöpt dissident groups and these know that in order to have any impact at all it is wise for them to maintain friendly relations with the PRI. Repression of uncoöptable groups is nowadays most of the time less harsh [this article was written before the 1968 and 1970 massacre of students and the 1971 insurrections in Mexico City and Guerrero], but it still exists.[30]

Mexico's growth rate and consequent social mobility have allowed a modicum of democracy. Mexico under the P.R.I. has not been Fascist Italy or Spain. In that Mexico has not resolved her perpetually sharp class antagonisms and faces serious stagnation, overpopulation, and therefore dissension problems in the coming decades, her system of presidential authoritism and corporate party structure remind me of inherent Fascist possibilities.

Conclusion

In conclusion, it would seem that the Mexican political system is approaching the breach, both ideologically and structurally. The growing concentration of wealth in the hands of the upper ranges of the middle class, the continuing heavy involvement of United States capital, an increasing number of poor people, continued corruption, and an educational system that serves too few too irrelevantly will certainly produce more strains, more open challenge and subversion, and therefore more bloody repression.[31] This is especially so in a global and epochal context of third-world liberation. In that Catholicism itself in Latin America is going through a revolution in which it is becoming much more aware of the need for temporal justice, this leftward move in the Church cannot help but affect Catholic thought and action in Mexico.

These strains and challenges strike out at a corporatism which many see as a castle wall erected by the new oligarchy to fend off the intensifying demands of an ever-growing popular class.

NOTES TO CHAPTER 4

1. Andre Gunder Frank, *Latin America: Underdevelopment or Revolution* (New York: Monthly Review Press, 1969), p. 300.

2. Frank, *Underdevelopment or Revolution,* pp. 306–7.

3. Ibid., p. 307.

4. Pablo Gonzales Casanova, "Mexico: The Dynamics of an Agrarian Semicapitalist Revolution," in *Latin America: Reform or Revolution?,* eds. James Petras and Maurice Zeitlin (New York: Fawcett World Library, 1968), p. 472.

5. Gonzales Casanova in *Reform or Revolution,* p. 469.

6. Gonzales Casanova, *La distribucion del ingreso y el desarrollo economico de Mexico* (Mexico: Escuela Nacional de Economia, 1960), p. 75; in Petras and Zeitlin, *Reform or Revolution,* p. 469.

7. Gonzales Casanova in *Reform or Revolution,* p. 469.

8. Frank, *Underdevelopment or Revolution,* p. 299.

9. Ibid., p. 300.

10. Fidel Castro, *History Will Absolve Me* (New York: Lyle Stuart, 1961), p. 33.

11. Frantz Fanon, *The Wretched of the Earth,* trans. Constance Farrington (New York: Grove Press, Inc., 1968), p. 37.

12. Henry Bamford Parkes, *A History of Mexico* (Boston: Houghton Mifflin Company, 1970), p. 151.

13. Fanon, *Wretched of the Earth*, pp. 54–55.

14. See Luigi Einaudi et. al., "Latin American Institutional Development: The Changing Catholic Church" (Rand Memorandum 6136–DOS, October 1969).

15. Francisco I. Madero, "Plan . . ." presented in *The Quest for Change in Latin America: Sources for a Twentieth Century Analysis,* eds. W. Raymond Duncan and James Nelson Goodsell (New York: Oxford University Press, 1970), p. 57.

16. Madero in *The Quest for Change,* p. 60.

17. Jose Vasconcelos, *Ulises Criollo* (Mexico, 1937), pp. 500–535; presented in *Readings in Latin American Civilization,* ed. Benjamin Keen (Boston: Houghton Mifflin Company, 1967), p. 356.

18. Vasconcelos in *Readings in Latin American Civilization,* p. 357.

19. John Womack, Jr., *Zapata and the Mexican Revolution* (New York: Vintage Books, 1968), p. 7.

20. See note 7.

21. Plan of Ayala presented in Womack, *Zapata and the Mexican Revolution,* p. 402.

22. Ibid.

23. Ibid., pp. 402–3.

24. Womack, *Zapata and the Mexican Revolution,* p. 393.

25. Howard F. Cline, *Mexico: Revolution to Evolution: 1940–1960* (New York: Oxford University Press, 1963), p. 123.

26. For a discussion of "authoritism," refer again to Francisco Jose Moreno, *Legitimacy and Stability in Latin America: A Study of Chilean Political Culture* (New York: New York University Press, 1969), pp. 23–27.

27. Fanon, *Wretched of the Earth,* p. 38.

28. Moreno, *Legitimacy and Stability,* p. 185.

29. See the P.N.R.-sponsored amendment to Article 3 of the Constitution in Duncan and Goodsell, *The Quest for Change,* pp. 100–102.

30. Anderson and Cockroft, "Control and Coöptation in Mexican Politics" in *Latin American Radicalism,* eds. Irving Louis Horowitz, Josue de Castro, and John Gerassi (New York: Vintage Books, 1969), p. 379.

31. For references to this situation, see Gustavo Diaz Ordaz, "State of the Union Address," of September 1, 1968, official English translation, pp. 5–7, 20–24, 27–28, 36–40 in Duncan and Goodsell, *The Quest for Change,* esp. pp. 121–22.

5
Chile:
Marx vs Thomas

This chapter will deal briefly with the political economy of Chile, a nation in which four-fifths of the population is economically and politically unenfranchised, i.e., on the margin of the economy and bereft of the possibilities of making any of the decisions which effect the national context of their lives. Second, I will explore the historic interplay between executive dominance and legalist limitations which preserves political stability but allows little inventiveness in dealing with Chile's tragic social and economic problems.

Last, and this with great trepidation in the face of the unknown, I will try to assess the possibilities arising from Chile's 1970 presidential election. I have decided that it would be more useful to present a theoretical discussion of the possibilities of Marxism in a Thomistic context and to avoid as much as possible the temptation to report and analyze day-to-day politics in Chile.[1] Given the context of national liberation struggles and international instability, Allende's victory might actually shatter Chile's antiquated and ineffectual Thomistic edifice, perhaps through very destructive civil war.

Political Stability and Its Price

Chile is a complex nation. It has achieved politically what no nation in Latin America, save Mexico, has achieved: it institutionalized political stability. The continuum of this stability has resulted in the election of a revolutionary Marxist. This political stability has been purchased at the price of social and economic regression and deprivation. The neo-Thomistic formula of Suarezian authorism and legalism had solidified the rule of a feudal-capitalist elite and the control of a large segment of the country's resources and infrastructure by North American imperialism.

The Factor of Income Distribution

The fact that Chile is considered one of the more advanced, modernized, and progressive nations in Latin America says that much less for the development of the continent. For an example of relative wealth and absolute poverty, Chile's per capita income ranks seventh in a listing of twenty-one western hemisphere nations. Her P.C.I. is $325, and this magnificent per capita reward is tempered by its distribution: 4.7% of the population, urban owners of capital, receive 39.3% of this national income. The distribution of income must also be considered in light of a consistent 18% unemployment rate. A running inflation of more than 25% over a long period of Chilean history has not only damaged savings and investment possibilities, but also robs the lower classes of the possibilities of economic relief.*

The dynamic of income distribution and differential is one in which the rich have been consistently getting richer and the poor more poverty-stricken. In comparing the income differential between such groups as businessmen and public administrators and their personal servants from 1940 to 1960, Petras finds that the former groups received a 52% increase while the latter suffered a decrease of 14%.[2]

A stroll through the streets of downtown Santiago quickly corroborates the existence and abuse of a rigid class society. Even the unaccustomed eye will be struck by the contrast between the well-dressed, well-fed *gente decente* and the shorter, poorly clothed, gap-toothed *roto,* "ragged one," as the urban worker is accurately called. Kalman Silvert characterizes this contrast well:

> This favored fifth comprises the effective Chilean nation. All public officials, military officers, intellectuals, professionals, bank clerks, store-keepers, industrialists and large farmers are recruited from this reduced but still significantly large segment. When we say "Chilean," the chances are almost absolute that it is to them we refer, unless we specifically say *roto* or *inquilino* or *callampa* dweller. Certainly when we comment on the beauty of Chilean women, we are not talking about the wives of farm workers; when we say Chilean governors are sophisticated, or that the Chilean diet is French, we are not referring to the political choices of illiterate peasants or the food eaten by a construction worker in Chillan. Granted, we always use such selective perceptions in talking about societies, but it is still useful to know that in Chile four-fifths of the population must be excluded from these generalizations.[3]

A large part of this lower four-fifths of the population live in Santiago. One-third of the 2.5 million inhabitants of that swelling city live in *poblaciones callampas* ("mushrooms," as the squatters' communities are called). This means that about 750,000 people live in huts of board, mud, and tin on land not wanted or temporarily abandoned, without running water, electricity, transportation, municipal garbage disposal, medical attention, or

*These figures and subsequent discussion of demography represent the pre-Allende situation. The tumultuous Allende period has not yet sorted itself out for analysis.

police protection. The more fortunate lower class live in *conventillos,* sparse, antiquated, overcrowded little rooms built around a courtyard.

Misuse of the Land

Land tenure and production figures help one to understand why the crush is so great in the city. Statistics for the 1960s indicate that 70% of Chile's cultivable land was owned by only 1.5% of the landowners. At the same time, 50% of the country's landowners held less than 1% of the land. The land concentrated in the hands of a few *terratenientes* was irrationally underutilized. Some of the big *fundos* devoted inordinate land and labor to the cultivation of grapes and artichokes, while some of the smaller operations grew wheat. Much of the land was neglected. While 1.1 million *hectares* were irrigated, only 785,000 were cultivated. This neglect is symptomatic of an atavistic basis of prestige, the land itself. Therefore mere ownership of a *fundo,* not its productivity, served as a basis of social status for an urban commercial or industrial entrepreneur. As a result of this neglect, a country which the Food and Agriculture Organization believes could feed 25 million people must export precious capital to import basic foods. Food shortage and speculation in food prices contribute to the inflationary spiral. Even the rich in this dietary dearth are deprived of fresh milk, as Santiago markets sell only powdered and reconstituted milk. Even wheat and potatoes are in short supply.

Change and Stagnation

The inequitable social and economic picture summarized above had not improved in through the period of the last presidential administration. Inflation remained high. Internal migration was still intense. Housing conditions worsened and all the indices of bleeding underdevelopment continued to characterize a society of political stability, apparent democracy, and great social injustice. However, to characterize Chilean society as static would be unfair and inaccurate.

Oswaldo Sunkel has called the Chilean dynamic basic change within the context of fundamental stagnation.[4] He cites a triad of important changes. Industrialization intensified during the world depression of the 1930s, and industrial production increased through the early 1950s so that industry produced a larger share of the national income and employed an increasingly larger proportion of the work force. This latter increase brought the industrial work force from 15.7% in 1930 to a significantly higher 24% in 1960. Income from the industrial sector increased from 13.8% to about 21.5% in the same period. As a consequence of this industrial surge, mining grew statistically less important. The income that Chileans derived from mining decreased from a high of 32.5% to below 5% of the national income.

Sunkel points out that the second important social change was a doubling of the population to 7.4 million. The increase in population growth from 1.4% to 2.4% was due mainly to a halving of the mortality rate from twenty-four per thousand in 1935 to twelve per thousand in 1960. This larger population shifted from the country to the city at an increasing rate. In 1960, two-thirds of Chile's people were concentrated in towns of over twenty thousand. Santiago's population more than doubled between 1930 and 1960 when it reached 2.5 million, representing one-third of the total population. The increased urban population reflects a smaller demand for workers in the nitrate fields, increased industrialization, and the stagnation of Chilean agriculture.

The third change, accompanying and partly encouraging the change in the economy and demography of Chile, was a large increase in government activities and an enlargement of the bureaucracy. This increase in activities and bureaucrats is reflected at all levels of Chilean government. The number of bureaucrats increased from the 1940 figure of 72,000 to 116,000 in 1955. Of the active population, 5.4% works for the national government. The greatest increases in government activity have been in economic development and health and welfare services.

Despite these ostensibly profound changes, the overall picture of the society has been one of stagnation. The causes of stagnation are hardly mysterious. Chile's principal wealth is copper; her mines contain 30% of the world's reserves and yield 25% of the world's production. Before the progressive nationalizations of Frei and Allende the entire copper industry was owned by American corporations, which remitted to the United States more that $120 million a year. (It might also be mentioned that profits soared to their highest levels after Frei's halfway house of "Chileanization.") This situation renders any talk of national planning so much rhetoric. Planning requires capital, and capital can be gotten only by petitioning the very sources that profit from underdevelopment. Chile was not a self-determining nation, but a subsidiary in a world-wide copper business.

The political apparatus, while growing, has grown to serve the already small entrepreneurial class more and more, thereby solidifying its hold on that part of the nation's economy not controlled by United States capital. The bureaucracy functioned in some cases to move lower middle class Socialists into the entrepreneurial upper middle class.[5] The potential progressive thrust of Chile's strong left is further blunted, Sunkel feels, by its concern with international affairs rather than the internal Chilean social dynamic.

Thus Chilean society was locked into a concentration of wealth, a nonproductive agriculture, and foreign domination of its major raw material. Its cities were intensively ruralized. Its political system was the servant of the domestic and foreign economic powers. It cannot be determined at this time whether or not Salvador Allende, leading a Marxist coalition, can break this rock of Chilean stagnation and injustice. A better understanding of Allende's possibilities can be achieved by studying the history of Chilean political development. The conclusion that emerges from such an examination is pessimistic. It states that the forms and processes which have gained legitimacy in Chile have served the small elite and therefore neglect and oppress the majority. If Allende perpetuates this tradition, by definition, his impact will be negative.

Historical Conflict Between Executive Dominance and Legalism

This evaluation of the Chilean presidency is not without paradox. Chile's constitution and its traditions allow for a powerful executive. Yet, one manifestation of the Thomist value structure, here termed "legalism," contributes to prevent that powerful executive from being the political innovator many in his country wish him to be. This section will discuss the historic interplay between executive dominance and legalist limitations which preserves political stability but allows little inventiveness in dealing with Chile's tragic social and economic problems.

It can be argued that if Thomism is as pervasive as I have suggested, then all countries in Latin America understand law in the same way. The question thus arises, why emphasize this particular aspect of the Thomist model in Chile? The answer is that Chile is one of the very few countries in Latin America to have discovered a consistent legitimacy. Between 1833 and the present, Chile has had two constitutions and three forms of government; two of them (one from 1833 to 1890 and another from 1920 to the present) were very similar in that they were dominated by the executive. This successful tradition of constitutionalism is thereby hallowed. This is so especially in relation to the rather sorry history of political instability in the rest of Latin America. Constitutional rule, that is, rule which does not violate constitutional latitude, is therefore inextricably intertwined with the Chilean's concept of his nation.

The Medieval Legacy

Legalism itself is the legacy of Spanish feudal order, of colonial political structures, and of the evolution of postrevolutionary politics. Legalism as a value structure was first postulated by medieval Catholic churchmen and exists today in both the rhetoric and the structure of the Chilean political system.

The basic proposition of legalism is that society and all its component structures are the expression of law. To repeat what has been defined in an earlier chapter, "law" here is used in its Thomistic sense. Specifically, law

is "an ordinance of reason made for the common good by the public personage who has charge of the community, and promulgated."[6] The reader will
recall that this promulgated ordinance of reason is not an isolated phenomenon in an atomic universe. The law for a particular community is an ultimate
reflection of eternal law. In fact, the universe and all its components are
united in that they are expressions of this eternal law.

> All things subject to divine providence are ruled and measured by the
> eternal law, and consequently it is clear that somehow they share in the
> eternal law, for under its influence they have their propensities to their
> appropriate activities and ends. Among all the rest, rational creatures
> most superbly come under divine providence, by adopting the plan and
> providing for themselves and for others. Thus they share in the eternal
> reason and responsibly pursue their proper affairs and purposes. This
> communication of the eternal law to rational creatures is called the
> natural law.[7]

These elements of law are further interconnected. Reason, from which
positive law emanates, is referred to by St. Thomas in the following way:
"The natural light of reason by which we discern what is right and wrong
is naught else but the impression on us of divine light."[8] Law is both divine
and perceivable to human beings. Therefore, it is incumbent upon man to
institute its form on earth. "All plans of inferior government should be
modelled on the eternal law, since it is the prototype. Hence Augustine says
that in temporal law, there is nothing just and lawful save what man has
drawn from the eternal law."[9]

According to Suarez, a leading post-medieval Spanish elaborator of St.
Thomas, not even the Pope can change natural law. This immutable law is
not only to rule within the state but is to dominate international relations.
"Thus it follows that states, like individuals, are subject to the law of nature,
a principle which implies the rule of law within the state and also legal
relations between states."[10]

Values Contained in Legalism

The task of this chapter will be to plot the development of this medieval
legacy through its Chilean evolution, from colonial structure to present-day
party politics. Before this can be done, the broader set of values contained
in legalism must be elaborated. When this has been accomplished, it should
be evident that Chilean politics is the product of a culture conditioned by
legalistic thinking. When President Jorge Alessandri's last foreign minister,
Julio Philippi, told this author that he is a Thomist, he stated in effect that
he is conscious of a cultural tradition born of medieval Catholic thought and
implanted in his mind by the enculturating processes of his society.[11] He
related that the Chilean can hold before him the utopian image of an or-

dered universe in a world which is either chaotic or threatening chaos. He can relegate the Hobbesian state of nature, in which a nation like Chile is powerless, to the realm of human inperfection. By attempting to institute a context of eternally sanctioned law, he not only provides the possibility of achieving a state of grace, but he can obviate the state of nature and enable the poor to dwell with the rich in a condition of Thomistic functional harmony.

From the idea of an ordered universe comes the concept of hierarchy. And from hierarchy comes the justification of authoritistic social and political leadership. This idea is crucial in understanding the process of political decision-making in Chile. Above the hue and cry of ostensible political pluralism is the authoritistic executive. This was implied in the Thomistic reference to the "public personage who *has charge* of the community."

Authoritism as a function of the strong executive has been well discussed and documented by Francisco Jose Moreno in his work, *Legitimacy and Stability in Latin America.*[12] However, in a very insightful work by Alberto Edwards Vives, another factor is added to the rule of authoritism.[13] In this book, Edwards credits the dominant aristocratic class with the leadership that was responsible for the tradition of peace and stability which has been the Chilean legacy. Both concepts, executive dominance and the dominance of a particular class, have had their day in Chile's history, have contributed to her stability, and thus hollowed, confirm the value of a hierarchical universe and its reflection in a hierarchical society.

The concepts of hierarchy and authoritistic leadership must be understood in viewing the leader's relationship to the law, to society, and to his source of power. One of the earliest Iberian contributors to the idea of a society dominated by its leader was the sixth-century Spanish bishop, San Isidro. According to Jaime Eyzaguirre,

> Two elements played harmoniously in the Isidorean political conceptualization: the king and the people. The investiture of the monarch is sacred; his power emanates from God. From here is drawn the prestige of his authority and the obligation of the people to support it.[14]

However, the king himself is encumbered by weighty responsibility. He is a very lonely leader, for between him and his subjects stands divine right, tempered, Eyzaguirre claims, by the excommunicative power of the church.[15] Thus the king is alone to discover the commandments of natural law. If he should rebel against the law, he would be a tyrant and subject to the anathema of the Church. Here we see that while the leader is above his society, he is not above the eternal hierarchy which reflects itself in law. These are the foundations of legalism. Constructed in the age of the Visigoths, they were finally transported to the New World. "The Spaniard during the course of the sixteenth and seventeenth centuries crossed the

Atlantic to settle himself in the new lands of America, possessing a multitude of perfectly structured political principles which . . . exhibit a long and well-founded genealogy."[16]

The Chilean Evolution of Legalism

Chile's colonial heritage preserved and promulgated the tradition built by San Isidro, St. Thomas, and the seventeenth-century Jesuits such as Suarez. The concept of the dominant leader limited within the bounds of legalism were planted in Chilean soil and flourished there. A number of factors were responsible for this. First, Chile was settled during the reign of one of Spain's most absolute, most popular, and, according to Luis Galdames, most beloved monarchs, Philip II.[17] He established a firm hierarchical administration which survived 300 years of use.

This hierarchy, with the crown firmly at the top, was supported by an almost equally powerful Church. In its inception under Philip II, Church-monarchy mutual support was fanatically pursued. Philip spent most of the wealth he derived from his colonies combatting the Reformation in Europe. The Church in turn exerted its tenacious hold on the colonies through the vehicle of the Inquisition. It did not, however, have to depend entirely on coercion, awesome as the punishments for heresy were. As Frank Tannenbaum points out:

> The Church was everywhere and with every individual all of his life. The day began with early morning mass and ended with an Ave Maria, and every occasion, every sorrow, every joy, every holiday, had its own special religious symbolism to be acted out in church. During the colonial period, the Church was also the school, the university, the hospital, the home for the aged, the sick, and the abandoned. It served the individual and the community in many ways.[18]

As the ubiquitous and powerful as the Church was in hierarchical colonial Chile, the king, through his administrators, still held sway. The Spanish crown, by virtue of Rome's acknowledged dependence on royal authority, had been granted powerful initiatives in Church business. The *Patronato Real* permitted the royal authorities to have the final word in the appointment of the colonial hierarchy, in the building of churches, and in the passage of any Church edicts relating to the colony. Although Luis Galdames believes that the Church became gradually superior to the political authority, from a structural point of view this was not exactly so.[19] Removal of legitimate royal authority with the Napoleonic sweep of Spain greatly undermined Church authority in the colonies. However, for the purposes of this discussion of the hierarchical expression of legalism in colonial Chile, the colony can be viewed as having dual pinnacles, each very powerful and each supporting the validity of hierarchy within a legal framework. The political hierarchy, with its royal dominance, was stronger because of the Church's world view. Although the Church shared authority with the viceroys and the captain-generals, the fundamental purity of a hierarchical universe was not violated because above these dual colonial pinnacles stood the king, with his primary but always legal relationship to God. The king's authority, delegated down through the hierarchy from the viceroy in Lima to the governor in Santiago, was manifold. The tradition of executive dominance had a powerful foundation in the royal representative. The governor, who also maintained the military title of capital-general, could command the army; appoint and remove public officials, except those appointed directly by the king; administer civil and penal justice as a supreme judge; direct the administration of cities; exercise the right of ecclesiastical patronage for the king; divide lands and Indians provisionally among individuals he thought most deserving; and as vice-patron of the Church, name the parish clergy.

It must be remembered that this dominant executive, with his impressive array of powers, existed within a context of laws which both limited and strengthened his authority. Within this legal schema, whoever felt that he was injured by the colonial administration could apply for justice to the Viceroy of Peru or directly to the king himself. The seemingly all-powerful governor was also subjected to a public hearing when his office terminated. All who had grievances against him came and presented them. These charges were reviewed in a hierarchical fashion. First, there was the hearing itself. The Council of the Indies then passed on the decisions of the local judging body. Finally, true to the system, the king himself decided the case. This stratified system survived for the three centuries of Spain's colonial rule. The success of Diego Portales in the nineteenth century, discussed later in this chapter, might lead to the conjecture that this complicated legal system actually strengthened the power of the governor. For within the context of the system, the governor and the king whom he represented became far more powerful than an arbitrary ruler could be. They were hallowed by the law and were therefore legitimate expressions of an eternal order.

This stress on law was a dominant feature of a colonial Chile just as it was shown in chapter 3 to be characteristic of the rest of colonial Spanish America. Here, as elsewhere, society was so structured that for its every facet there was a legal code and a judge. Chile, typical of Spanish colonies, suffered the monopoly over intellectual input and development exercised by the Church throughout the Imperium. Likewise, the devastating intellectual products of the Reformation and enlightenment were edited out of the Chilean experience by the omniscient Holy Office.

The isolation imposed on Chile by Spanish mercantilism (discussed earlier) was heightened by Chile's natural isolation. She was cut off by impassable mountains in the east, desert in the north, and dense forest lands populated by the fierce Araucanian Indians in the south. These barriers combined to prohibit even illegal trade with her neighbors. Internal conditions were no better. During the colonial period roads, where they existed at all, were in very poor repair. The principal trade route was between Santiago and Valparaiso, a distance of less than 100 miles through hill country. This trip, which can be made in a couple of hours today, took several days on mule or horseback. Chile's two major centers of activity remained almost isolated from each other as well as from the rest of the world.

The colonial period in Chile lasted 300 years. During that time, Chile lived within the legalistic context of order, hierarchy, and authoritism. Its intellect was molded by the medieval teachings of the Church and the colonial structure imposed by an absolute monarch. The world view which emerged from this experience was insulated from the corrupting influences of the European intellectual ferment by a strict policy of mercantilism and the natural isolation of its rugged terrain.

When the Spanish monarchy was inundated by the Napoleonic wave in 1810, the colonial edifice was shaken. Chile was left a body without a head. The pinnacles of the social hierarchy were removed. Chile, conditioned to obey a king who derived his authority from God, was asked to pay allegiance to a monarch established by a French revolutionary government whose God was Reason. For over 20 years, Chile floundered in chaos. She had survived for 300 years on an order confirmed by faith and authority. With faith shaken and legitimate authority unavailable, the Chilean Republican experiment was a failure. Legitimate authority was usurped for more than a decade (c. 1817–1835) by a series of *caudillos*. The *caudillo* was authoritarian enough. He failed because his authority was grounded in personality and brute force instead of law.

Legalism and Stability

The disorder lasted until the ingredients of Chilean stability were rediscovered and the political system was restructured according to the dictates of this legalistic recipe. Ironically, Diego Portales, who was responsible for this return to stability, never held the presidency. His rule, like his formula for order, was impersonal.[20]

> A man of intuition, Portales understood the necessity of giving a social foundation to the political structure, of grouping all social forces in support of an impersonal regime of legitimate tradition which could offer legal regularity, decorum, and circumspection, a guarantee of order, and finally, good government. To Portales, constitutional techniques were only accessory; the essential issue was to set up what he called "the mainspring of the machinery": traditional authority, a quiet

and silent force, loyally obeyed and respected, eternal above any *caudillos* and factions.[21]

The Constitution of 1833

Portales accomplished this by restoring authority within a legal context. The Constitution of 1833, with its provisions for autocratic rule, returned Chile to the monarchical and aristocratic tradition of the colonial period. The fact that Chile remained outwardly republican gave the political system a new type of nineteenth-century legitimacy, while reestablishing an order forged in medieval Spain. According to Federico Gil,

> Chile became an exception among the former Spanish colonies, enjoying political stability precisely because of having preserved intact its colonial past. It was in this sense socially the most backward of them all.[22]

A series of powerful executives ruled Chile from the inception of the Constitution of 1833 until 1891.[23] However, the king-president was not the sole mainstay of Chilean stability. For Chile was not only ruled by an autocratic executive; she was also dominated by a strict but flexible hierarchy.[24] This hierarchy was strict in the sense that class was and still is an important social and political determinant in Chile. However, a certain flexibility manifested itself in the economic composition of the hierarchy. The *Fronda Aristocratica,* the dominating class in Chilean society, contained members of the old colonial aristocracy and recent arrivals who had succeeded in commerce and industry. This combination of social and economic groups obviated one of the basic elements of conflict in society. The old feudal class, preserving totally the traditions of order, simply absorbed the new financially powerful groups and imposed upon them an entire value structure. This amalgamation and value adaption has inhibited the modernization of Chile, but it has also preserved relatively unchallenged the social reflection of an orderly universe.

It should not be understood that the originator of this legalistic concept of order, the Catholic Church, remained unchallenged through this century of Chilean republicanism. Within the context of Chilean politics there did arise political parties of some influence which challenged the relationship between church and state. However, after 300 years of Catholic ubiquity, the Church itself as a formal body involved in politics was no longer necessary to preserve a value structure. Legalism had become a part of lay thought. The success of Portales's solution showed that the Catholic formula for stability was inherent in the Chilian social order.

Portales's conception of an orderly society, welded together by an autocratic executive who based his power on the support of the ruling class, survived for almost the entire nineteenth century. Presidential dictatorship outlasted the separation of church and state and the rise of new commercial groups. The combination of a ruling elite and its dictatorial representative surviving as it did over a long period, had a lasting effect on the stability of Chilean society.

Rebellion Against Legalism

In 1891 a certain tension which has existed for some time in Chile between members of the aristocracy translated itself into a successful rebellion against presidential authority. The issues involved were certainly not those of a pluralistic, participant political system. This was a monarchical-feudal struggle which characterized the Europe of an earlier age. When Jose Manuel Balmaceda, the last of the king-presidents for a number of decades to come, attempted to defend his position, he made an ironic appeal. This autocrat, a living reason for the quiescence of the majority of the Chilean populace, appealed for popular support. "When Balmaceda, in the anguish of the final battle with feudalism, wished, like the kings of old in Europe, to appeal to the people, to democratic sentiment, events proved that the ill-fated President had requested the protection of something which did not exist."[25]

The nonexistence of the populace as a political force and the well-entrenched legalism of the ruling class prevented an immediate rupture in the essential order of Chilean society. The presidency lost almost all of its power, but the oligarchy through its social and economic power maintained relative stability. When this backlog of order finally dissipated in the squabble of many meaningless political parties and first risings of the lower classes, Chile reverted in part to the Portales prescription of authority.

Revival of the Legalist Tradition

In 1920, Arturo Alessandri, "The Lion of Tarapaca," was elected President of Chile.[26] The deterioration of order in Chilean politics and the inability of the leaderless system to handle the problems which threatened stability reawakened the desire for an authoritistic solution. After a last-ditch revolt by the parliamentary oligarchy was defeated by the army, Alessandri effected a new presidential constitution in 1925. Legalism was revived. Authority would be exercised within the context of law. The 1925 constitution reestablished what Mario Bernaschina has called "legal autocracy."[27] An ironic feature of Chilean legalism as it relates to this legal autocrat is that it allows him to rule extralegally. For example, the president may rule by an extraconstitutional instrument called a "decree with the force of law."[28] Under this decree power, the president can have the Congress delegate part of its own law-making authority to him. He also enjoys considerable fiscal power. His money bill becomes law automatically if the Congress does not act on it within four months.[29] In an emergency, declared by himself, he can appropriate extra funds by decree.

An interesting feature of the legalist mentality that limits the efficacy of the president has been the refusal of Chilean chief executives to be excessive in their use of power. They have not violated the essential legal structure of the society as they interpreted it to wage campaigns of sweeping reform. Thus the legal autocrat is essentially a conservative force, no matter what political party he represents.

Carlos Ibanez, who assumed the presidency in 1952, acted in the light of this legalistic restriction.[30] Ibanez was, by Chilean standards, a charismatic leader. He was an army general and had even usurped the presidency illegally. He was, for the Chilean electorate in 1952, the strong man who was going to create a revolution from above, in the style of Juan Perón. He was expected to be the force, untainted by parliamentary squabbles, that could find solutions for a society beset by social and economic problems. Ibanez did nothing of the sort. Although he did not sell the presidency short, he stayed within the limits of traditional expectations.

Jorge Alessandri Rodriguez was a leader similar to Ibanez in that he was the man above politics. He was hallowed by age, dignity, and austerity. Little changed under his hand, but he held back the tide and preserved the legal order. His decisions were regarded as his own and above the fracas of partisan politics. He is much admired in Chile as a true product and practitioner of the legalist way.

The outcome of the heated contest between Christian Democracy and the Marxist coalition (F.R.A.P.)[31] in the 1964 presidential election underscores the durability of the legalist tradition.[32] Christian Democracy emphasized that it was going to bring about the badly needed revolution, but that this revolution was going to take place in a context of liberty. Translated into the practices of the Chilean political system, revolution in liberty means that the Christian Democrats were setting out to reform society without cracking the traditional mold of order, hierarchy and authority. Their ideal was not egalitarian society, but a society in which the classes cooperate and the social hierarchy remains.[33] The revolution the Chileans feared was the Cuban type, which they believed would follow a F.R.A.P. victory.[34] Christian Democracy's electoral success was based on a program that is essentially Thomism in twentieth-century dress.[35] The basic documents of Christian Democratic thought are Pope Leo XIII's *Rerum Novarum* and Pius XI's *Quadregisimo Anno*. The philosopher of Christian Democracy is the French neo-Thomist Jacques Maritain.[36] Chilean society, as it was to be ideally reformed by Eduardo Frei, was to reflect the truth of eternal order.

An irony of Chilean politics is that the Frapistas themselves as parliamentary parties have long been playing an unrevolutionary game, totally respectful of stability and order.[37] The Chilean Communist Party grew out of a leftist grouping formed in 1912. Since that time, the party has been markedly unrevolutionary and very much within the institutional mold of legislative politics. Nothing in the 1964 F.R.A.P. platform indicated that they were going to undermine basic political institutions and practices.[38] The fear of leftist aims expressed by the electorate came more from rightist propaganda and the example of Cuba than from the actual F.R.A.P. program.

A Lasting Tradition

To underscore the lasting presence of the legalist tradition, it would be interesting to inspect the writings of two modern Chilean political theoreticians. Jorge Ivan Hubner Gallo presents the conservative position. He condemns Christian Democracy for being too liberal and at the same time a handmaiden of communism.[39] His principal contention is that social justice must be administered paternalistically, within a stratified, closed society. He criticizes the Christian Democrats for thinking of the rights of the individual rather than of the Thomistic "common good."

> They do not contemplate organizing suffrage upon a logical, hierarchical basis . . . nor are they willing to place upon liberty the restraints demanded in the interest of moral goodness and truth. Their ideology rests neither upon the glorious Aristotelian-Thomistic tradition, nor upon pontifical teachings.[40]

The legalist tradition is clearly stated as Hubner presents the philosophical underpinnings of conservatism.

> On our part, we think that the ideological basis of traditional conservatism is epitomized in three great concepts which together constitute the prerequisite conditions for all progress. All three are rooted in natural reason and natural law. These are the concepts of God, State, and Social Order.[41]

Finally, Hubner presents the principles of the ideal conservative regime.

> Only an authoritarian, honest, impersonal and efficient regime, which does not represent the majority, but rather the best, can instill in the masses a sense of obedience and implant in the social life the principles of order, hierarchy, and discipline, which are indispensable for attaining the common good and rational progress.[42]

Eudardo Frei Montalvo presents the argument of the Christian Democrats.[43] One cannot help but notice in Christian Democratic rhetoric references to the same constants which motivate conservative thought. The emphasis for the Christian Democrat is more on progress, but the vocabulary is Aristotelian-Thomistic. "Only Christianity can provide the basis adequate to stimulate the majority of Chileans to work for the common good," says Frei.[44]

Frei goes on to comment on the dilemma of modern man living out his life as a lonely individual out of the context of order. "Then, [after the triumph of Christian Socialism] the man trembling in the night will be replaced by a citizen who can feel a sense of participation in the community and who can understand that he is part of a great family."[45]

The use of the word "family" is important, for the Christian Democrat thinks of society not as a collection of individuals but as a group of functional organisms. "The action of the state," writes Frei," . . . must respect intermediate organisms—the family, the city, the region, the trade union, the business enterprise. It must exert an effective authority for orientation, planning, and leadership."[46] The important things are law, organicism, and leadership, all within the context of what Frei terms a "spiritual hierarchy."[47]

Frei claims that inequity of laws explains "how a nation can cease to be an organic whole."[48] He goes on to underscore the importance of leadership within the context of common motives.

> If our country lacks common motives, it also lacks leaders who know how to lead and who have the moral integrity that is necessary to command respect and to impose constructive norms. We lack the spiritual hierarchy of values which must underlie effort that is generally conducive to the common good. . . . In summary, we do not feel the presence of the kingdom of justice among ourselves.[49]

Hubner and Frei represent the supposed opposite positions of reaction and reform, yet the two ideologies contain a number of identical principles. Both are products of medieval legalism perpetuated throughout history as an essential part of Chilean culture.

The chapter has described the development of Chilean legalism. Emanating as a world view in the sixth century under the influence of San Isidro, chrystalized in the writings of St. Thomas Aquinas, the idea of the legal hierarchy was firmly planted in Latin America during the conquest and colonial era. When Diego Portales "discovered" the Chilean social reality and embodied that reality in the lasting Constitution of 1833, the legal paliative for an ordinarily chaotic world was reaffirmed as a durable part of the Chilean political culture. Chilean adherence to the value of legal norms allowed for the popularity of Christian Democracy and its promise to bring fundamental change while preserving the legal structure of the state and making this fundamental change a reflection of moral truth.

In the final analysis, Chilean legalism is a response to the potential chaos inherent in an inequitable society and a rationalization of the need to revolutionize the structure of that society.

Progress Under the Christian Democrats

Although Christian Democracy promised much, six years of rule seemed to accomplish little. A dynamic world of ever-intensifying contradictions was confirmed for Chile. In that Frei would not violate the norms of legalism or tamper with the tradition of constitutional presidents, his administration moved forward much more slowly than Chile's woes. Therefore, even though some of the Frei programs seemed ambitious at the beginning of the Christian Democratic incumbency, each of them had to struggle through a recalcitrant, politically competitive, bourgeois legislature. Six years of struggle and compromise merely to legislate programs left an impatient country far from the cures and new starts Chileans desired.

Frei's Accomplishments

The statistics of Frei's accomplishments are indeed depressing, given the promises that swept him into office in 1964. The inflation had reached 33% in 1967, and the economy registered a growth rate of 1.5% compared to the steady 5.1% accomplished under the conservative hand of Jorge Alessandri. The core of the Christian Democratic promise had been agrarian reform. After struggling for two-and-a-half years to wrench a law from Congress, extremely little was done to translate the law into practice. The family resettlement program pledged during the election campaign and at the beginning of Christian Democratic reign spoke of resettling 100,000 families. This was a modest figure when it is noted that 350,000 agricultural families are landless. After reducing this promise a number of times, fewer than 20,000 families had been resettled as of 1969. Again, Chile had an ambitious agrarian reform law, the second within the decade, but little to show for the result of the legislative game.

Equally poor progress was made in housing construction. The alleviation of a housing deficiency of 600,000 units was not even attempted during Frei's incumbency. Christian Democracy promised a start of 360,000 housing units but settled for more modest yearly projections. The highest of these was 59,000 in 1967 and it was not even half achieved with 22,000 units. Low-income housing, which did not interest the private builders who took advantage of government loans, suffered most. The year 1966 saw only 8,500 low-income units built out of a projected 40,000. In 1967 only one-eighth of the low-income houses planned were actually built. The record of six years of Christian Democracy shows relatively more middle- and upper-income housing built than lower-income dwellings. In order to finance faltering programs of social reform, more foreign investment was encouraged. This greater foreign investment, combined with a faltering agricultural sector, more food imports, and greater consumer demands by a more affluent few in the middle and upper sectors, all spelled greater deprivation for Chile's suffering majority.

Frei accomplished this triumph by playing the game in the traditional manner. He promised to realize the Thomist communitarian idea without destroying the old reality. Frei was in the line of strong charismatic leaders without the power to change the social and economic picture. In that he used a political apparatus fixed to benefit the top fifth of Chilean society and therefore to oppress the bottom four-fifths, the results of his incumbency were predictable. Legalism, the exaltation of form and denigration of practice, lubricated a system in which dissent and insurgency are channeled, moderated, and therefore negated by the system's operation. The legislature obstructed, and the bureaucracy, Socialists and Radicals among them, rewarded a wealthy clientele. Frei's failures are the failures of a system. Frei fulfilled the requirements of leadership within that system. Moreno discounts the appeal of Christian Democratic ideology in Frei's electoral success.

> The victory of Frei has been commonly explained in terms of his party's ideology and platform. Such an explanation implies a high degree of rational behavior on the part of the voters, and it is usually more representative of the analyst's intellectual preconceptions and political orientation than of reality. An electorate that had chosen Carlos Ibanez and Jorge Alessandri on the basis of their caudillistic personalities could not have been changed in so short a period of time. It is true that the Christian Democratic party had been gaining in strength steadily since it changed its name in 1957, but its rapid advance was more the result of the caudillistic image of its leader than the objective value of its philosophy.[50]

Social, Economic, and Political Changes

Moreno implies that the system perpetuates and sustains its own kind of authority. However, to consider this a perpetual, static truth is also an unsupported assumption. One could also perceive Chile as changing. Oswaldo Sunkel's analysis, discussed earlier, contains the indices of that change, even though Sunkel concludes, as Moreno does, that Chile has been and remains a society which is in a fundamental way unchanging. The Election of Salvador Allende might contradict both pessimistic analyses. Although Allende's percentage of the vote remained fairly constant in the three previous elections (about 36%), the presidential election of 1970 changed that quantitative consistency into qualitative change. Allende rode to power supported by a militant and organized labor sector which has traditionally supported the left. In addition, his victory was backed by a newly self-conscious section of society. The Chilean peasantry in greater numbers are breaking out of their deferential torpor and demanding payment on the promises of agrarian reform made by both Alessandri and Frei. During Frei's presidency, the peasants, believing they were licensed by the Christian Democratic programs, began on a number of occasions to make their own expropriations. Petras states that the number of peasants involved in strikes tripled between 1964 and 1965.[51] He credits this new responsiveness of the peasantry to agricultural mechanization.

> In recent years several trends have contributed to undermining the traditional patterns of authority and social relations in the countryside. These trends are increased communications among peasants and between the peasants and sources promoting agrarian reform; growing corporate ownership of agriculture; mechanization of production and specialization of labor; the replacement of payments in kind by cash payments; migration of peasants to the cities; and communication of agriculture.[52]

These social and economic changes, including increased social differentiation, translated into political impact, mean increased political awareness and radicalization. This radicalization, expressing itself in left-wing voting and increased militancy, result from the contradiction between these pregnant changes and the continued stagnation of agricultural productivity and opportunity.

Frei contributed to this progressive dynamic by attempting to unionize the peasantry under the banner of his own party. While I was in Chile, I witnessed the interesting spectacle of hundreds of *campesinos* being led through the streets of Santiago to the Moneda Palace by Christian Democratic cadre in support of the president's agrarian unionization bill. The peasants paraded through the streets looking more bewildered by the city than enthusiastic, but this was a beginning. The Christian Democratic effort at mobilization resulted in the small *Unión de Campesinos de Chile*. It was a response to and in competition with growing Communist approaches and organization in the countryside. The left's discovery of the peasant, especially the growing agricultural proletariat, occurred during the election campaigns of 1958 and 1964. More recently, the militant M.I.R. *(Moviemiento Izquierdista Revolucionario)* has been working in the country organizing, arming the peasants, and encouraging collective expropriation of their *fundos*. Whereas Frei on many occasions moved against these precipitous land takeovers, Allende so far has not.

This new revolutionary constituency in the countryside is swelled by the politicization of the *callampistas.* These rural expatriates have been mobilized by the Christian Democratic left, and here again M.I.R. moved in, capitalizing on the unfulfilled promises of establishment parties, and attempted to create both an armed militia and a sanctuary for themselves for times when they were being pursued by the police.

The total effect of this political bombardment was to create greater support for Allende in his 1970 campaign and to bring the peasantry and lumpen proletariat into the Chilean political crucible.

The emergence of these two groups and the earlier emergence of militant industrial workers, accompanied by the consistent strength of the political left, lead one to believe that a qualitative change might be possible for Chile. Salvador Allende's election alone does not prove that this change has taken place. However, Allende's support is growing more radical and his program is creating a base for mass mobilization which has allowed him to make a considerable assault on Chilean feudal-capitalism. This attack may well result in qualitative changes. In his assaults so far, Allende's ranks have been joined by many young Christian Democrats who do not consider themselves Marxists but who have been influenced by Marx and Lenin's analyses of capitalism and imperialism.[53] It should be noted that a formally constituted segment of revolutionary Catholicism, and M.A.P.U. *(Movimiento de Acción Popular Unido)* led by Jacques Chonchol, has defected from the Christian Democratic party to join Allende's *Unidad Popular.* A new fragment of revolutionary Christian Democracy has since obtained Chonchol's leadership. It calls itself the Christian Left.

Future of the Revolution

The future of the Chilean "revolution" would seem to hang on three critical points of the Basic Program of the Popular Unity government. All of these points fall under "Political Reorganization" and "Judicial Reform." The first point is to replace the Chilean parliamentary system with a "People's Assembly" on a national and local level with the purpose of eliminating dictatorial presidentialism and vicious parliamentarianism.

A second critical point is contained in the plan to decentralize the bureaucratic national system by giving to regional and local organizations economic, social, and political power; also they will be allowed to have a voice and to criticize the actions of the superior institutions.

As for judicial reform, the U.P. would create a Supreme Court appointed by the People's Assembly, "with no limitation but the honesty of its members; thus replacing the current personalistic and bourgeois system"[54]

Difficulty of Change Through
the Legalistic System

These aims seem to spell the difference between the stagnation of legalism and the dynamic of revolution because nowhere has it been truer than in Chile that "the state is an organ of class rule, an organ for the oppression of one class by another; it is the creation of 'order,' which legalizes and precipitates this oppression by moderating the conflict between the classes."[55] As has been pointed out above, Chilean state power is expressed through a powerful yet legalistically conformist presidency, a compromising, obstructionist parliament, and a bureaucracy which serves as a hall of favors for the wealthy. All of this is in the face of an increasingly conscious, oppressed majority and an increasingly regressive economy. One must doubt the ability of any Marxist revolutionary to create profound social change using this classic status quo state apparatus. Frei promised a "Revolution in Liberty." As was shown, this promise was cancelled by the compromises and opportunism encouraged by this very same state apparatus. It performed its system maintenance function well, despite the Christian Democratic faith that the system could be an instrument of change.

It is difficult to understand how any attempt to abolish this state structure and replace it with a popular structure can be accomplished through the legalistic structure itself. Chile's long history of political stability as the context of distributive and participatory injustice substantiates the Marxist-Leninist assertion that the state is the product of the irreconcilability of class antagonisms. Its purpose is to maintain an unjust order which serves the interests of the class which had the power to create it. An apparatus custom-built by one class to oppress another can hardly be a weapon of liberation. It is a gun with a fixed position which must be destroyed when the oppressed want to liberate themselves. This is not a call to arms on the part of this writer—it is simply an analysis of the narrow possibilities inherent in an attempt to revolutionize Chilean society. Centers of violent opposition to Allende's presidency and the U.P. program already exist and have demonstrated their power. There are continued and well-founded reports that the right is increasingly well-armed and well-organized.

It would seem natural that a ruling class as comfortable and well-entrenched as Chile's is not going to surrender hundreds of years of customary perquisites and privileges without a fight. This is even more so because the Chilean oligarchy has been characterized and characterizes itself as a class that is flexible and willing to compromise. Their technique has been intelligent flexibility in the face of challenge. They have demonstrated this flexibility both on the legislative front (viz., Jorge Alessandri's Agrarian Reform Law of 1962) and in relation to Chilean social structure. In this area, the old *Fronda* has opened its ranks to the commercial and industrial groups of the nineteenth century. It has never frowned on co-opting through marriage an intelligent upstart of lower-middle class origins. Eduardo Frei, for example, is the son of a lower-middle class Swiss immigrant family, but he surmounted this obstacle to success in his marriage to the daughter of the well-established, wealthy Taglia family.

This compromising stance has heightened the Chilean ruling class's sense of *noblesse oblige.* Unlike the rigid neighboring oligarchies in Peru and Argentina, the Chilean upper class has been willing to bend and make sacrifices to maintain its position. And this is all the more reason for self-righteous outrage at a genuine threat to its existence.

Weaknesses of the Left

With peasants effecting *de facto* agrarian reform, with no defense of privilege in the judiciary and no salvation in an ideologically compromising and co-opting legislature, with no channel of influence in the bureaucracy and no shield in the legalistic presidency, the oligarchy would be left institutionally defenseless. The transformation of this oligarchic paraphernalia into a popular government would mean the end of privilege. But the Thomistic hierarchy has not toppled yet, and it has a long non-revolutionary past to support it. Where its own strengths fail, there is a potential weakness of the opposition.

The first of these status quo possibilities was exemplified by the unstable nature of the initial U.P. coalition. Both the ideological commitment to revolution and the class composition of the parties involved differed enough to pose a danger to cooperation in the face of intensified opposition or a too partisan stance by Allende. The coalition was also endangered by the possibility of Allende's moving too slowly and getting bogged down in the Chilean legislative miasma. An inspection of the parties in the winning U.P. coalition in the light of recent Chilean history brings home the difficulty of party alliances as a revolutionary instrument.

The first U.P. Cabinet consisted of four major groups and two smaller ones. (1) Allende's Socialist party is a grouping of socialist splinters with a history of dissolution and reformation. It draws its strength from the urban working class; however, it contains a large contingent of lower-middle-class and intellectual members. The party has been characterized as both nationalistic and revolutionary.[56] It is perhaps the most militant group in the U.P.

(2) The Communist party of Chile is a largely working-class party. It is the best organized and the most disciplined party in Chile. Its roots are old, going back to Recabarren's 1912 Workers' Socialist Party. In 1921 this Workers' Socialist Party joined the Third International, accepted the line of the Communisty Party U.S.S.R., and since 1956, consistent with its allegiance to the Soviet party, has followed the ideological line of "the peaceful road to socialism." In contradistinction to this line, it is hard to see the Communists defecting if they see revolution materializing in Chile. It would

probably be their hope to have strong influence and even to lead in a revolutionary effort. However, if the example of other Latin Communist parties (like the *Partido Socialista Popular* of Cuba) has any meaning, the Chilean Communists would want some guarantee of revolutionary success before they decide they have no other choice but to be deeply involved. But unlike their Cuban counterparts, the P.C.Ch. has been waging the battle of illegal expropriation in the countryside, encouraging peasant takeovers. The Communists have also established Committees of Popular Unity throughout the country, building local power as an alternative to constitutional bourgeois power. Whether this independent action will rent the U.P. coalition is difficult to judge at this point. The Communists and Socialists show a graph of conflict and cooperation. The P.C.Ch. involvement in the Popular Front of 1938–1941 was a Macchiavellian attempt to steal the workers' movement from the Socialists. Following the instruction of the Comintern, the party did not join the Popular Front. Instead they backed its election and continuously railed against the Socialists for the failures of the coalition. The 1958 election found the P.C.Ch. joined with the Socialists in F.R.A.P. as the *Frente* narrowly missed winning that election from Jorge Alessandri. In the parliamentary game of threat, bargain, and concession, the Communists and Socialists temporarily dissolved F.R.A.P. before the 1970 election and the Communists offered the very distinguished but unlikely candidacy of Pablo Neruda.

(3) The Radical party is a political grouping that has perpetually looked both right and left. From the decade of the 1940s to the election of 1958, the Radicals maintained a right of center stance. However, their middle-class ranks have been rent by the contradictions within that class. As a result, a strong segment of the party's younger intellectuals stood with the left. Members of this leftist faction cooperated with Allende in 1964 to write F.R.A.P.'s OCEPLAN, the economic program of the coalition. At the same time, the rightist grouping put forth the candidacy of Julio Duran, to oppose both Allende and Frei. It is difficult to say how this pragmatic grouping will wear over a long, Radical haul. It is very possible that an increasingly revolutionary situation might force new splits in the party rather than a wholesale withdrawal.

(4) As was mentioned before, M.A.P.U. was the newest of the large constellations in U. P. It is a left Christian Democratic movement and represents the great dissatisfaction with Frei's "Revolution in Liberty" which I found among Christian Democratic youth as early as 1965. It was originally headed by the progressive agrarian reformer, Jacques Chonchol, who obtained the agriculture portfolio in Allende's cabinet. The question mark here is ideological as well as a matter of power politics. Although Chonchol was able to work with Castro on the Cuban agrarian reform program, it is difficult to determine whether Thomistic communitarianism as Chronchol and Silva conceived it in their *Hacia Mundo Sociedad Comunitario* will ultimately be compatible with socialism in power as it evolves in Chile.

The other two groups in the U.P. were the tiny Social Democratic party and the also small *Accion Popular Independiente,* which contributed constituency and parliamentary strength to the coalition.

It would seem from this conglomerate of social and ideologically disparate groupings that this coalition would be a difficult phalanx with which to move radically into the future. In fact, the coalition did crack under the pressure of political exigency and parliamentary pressure. A number of new coalitions have been formed and dissolved, including, at times, a member of the military.

It must also be kept in mind that this first coalition took power in the routine of elections. An electoral campaign has considerably less momentum and is considerably less significant than a revolutionary seizure of power. The latter situation, as represented in the Soviet, Chinese, and Cuban cases, tests both the revolutionary commitment of the new power group and the readiness of the society for radical change. Neither of these factors is so apparent in today's Chile.

The objective conditions of economic stagnation and social repression, salient as they have been in the last decades, do not insure a subjective triumph over the imperialistically and oligarchically supported Thomistic legalism of the past. If the Chilean army moves to protect this tradition and its base of privilege before counter institutions and ideology are sufficiently strong, the result might be civil war or reaction.

This has by no means been a full catalog of factors protecting Chile's oligarchy. The most obvious omission is the United States. The loss of Indochina and the introduction of communism to South America would not be too palatable for the United States. Even if Chile's copper can be replaced by other world sources and the investment climate seems more favorable in other countries, the strategic position of Chile as a possible leftist base bordering Peru, Bolivia, and Argentina and the significance of an early defiance of North American suzerainty might be too much for an American president to bear. At present, it would seem that the forbearance of the United States is based on internal obstacles to revolution as well as nationalistic divisiveness in southern South America. It was predicted in a 1965 issue of *Punto Final* entitled *¡Golpe de Estado en Chile!* that the massing of Peruvian, Bolivian, and Argentine troops along the Chilean border would provoke the Chilean army into a coup, if the internal situation threatened legalism.

Conclusion

It can be concluded from this appraisal of Chile's present and an appreciation of her all too stable past that the road to a new society is not clear. Given an increasingly deteriorating objective environment, the ultimate hurdle will be the extremely durable superstructure of legalistic practices and Thomistic ideas.

NOTES TO CHAPTER 5

1. A number of writers have taken on this task. One notable example is James Petras, whose very incisive article, "The Transition to Socialism in Chile: Perspectives and Problems," appeared in the *Monthly Review,* October 1971.

2. These are subsequent figures unless otherwise indicated are quoted from James Petras, *Politics and Social Forces in Chilean Development* (Berkeley and Los Angeles: University of California, 1961), chap. 1, pp. 6–36.

3. Ralman Silvert, *Chile: Yesterday and Today* (New York: Holt, Rinehart & Winston, 1965), p. 27.

4. This discussion is found in Sunkel's "Change and Frustration in Chile," in *Obstacles to Change in Latin America,* ed. Claudio Veliz (London: Oxford University Press, 1969), pp. 116–44.

5. For an extensive analysis of the Chilean bureaucracy, see Petras, *Politics and Social Forces,* chap. 8, pp. 288–337.

6. St. Thomas Aquinas, *Philosophical Texts,* ed. Thomas Gilbey (New York: Oxford University Press, 1960), p. 354.

7. St. Thomas, *Philosophical Texts,* p. 358.

8. Ibid.

9. Ibid.

10. George Sabine, *A History of Political Theory,* 3d ed. (New York: Holt, Rinehart & Winston, 1961), p. 391.

11. Author's interview with Julio Philippi, November 17, 1965.

12. The full title of Moreno's work is *Legitimacy and Stability in Latin America: A Study of Chilean Political Culture* (New York: New York University Press, 1969). See especially pp. 23–27.

13. Alberto Edwards Vives *La Fronda Aristocratica* (Santiago: Ediciones Ercilla, 1936).

14. Jaime Eyzaguirre, *Idearioy Ruta de la Emancipacion Chilena* (Santiago: Editorial Universitaria, 1957), p. 15.

15. Ibid.

16. Ibid.

17. Luis Galdames, *A History of Chile,* trans. Isaac Joslin Cox (Chapel Hill, N.C.: The University of North Carolina Press, 1941), p. 61.

18. Frank Tannerbaum, *Ten Keys to Latin America* (New York: Random House, 1962), p. 57.

19. Galdames, *History of Chile,* p. 66.

20. For an authoritative biography of Portales, see Francisco A. Encina, *Portales* (Santiago: Editorial Nacimiento, 1934).

21. Federico G. Gil, *The Political System of Chile* (Boston: Houghton Mifflin Company, 1966), p. 37.

22. Ibid., p. 39.

23. See Federico G. Gil, *Genesis and Modernization of Political Parties in Chile* (Gainsville: University of Florida Press, 1962).

24. Edwards, *La Fronda Aristocratica, passim.*

25. Ibid., p. 179.

26. An interesting analysis of Alessandri's reign is found in Moreno, *Legitimacy and Stability*, pp. 149–61.

27. For a detailed discussion of the Constitution of 1925, see Mario Bernaschina G., *La Constitucion Chilena* (Santiago de Chile: Editorial Juridica, 1957).

28. Ibid., pp. 26–28.

29. Chile, Constitution, Article 44.

30. Gil, *The Political System*, p. 77.

31. *Frente de Accion Popular* was the Socialist-Communist coalition.

32. For a detailed account of the 1964 election, see Federico G. Gil and Charles J. Parrish, *The Chilean Presidential Election of September 4, 1964: Part I* (Washington: ICOPS, 1965).

33. Frederick B. Pike, *Chile and the United States, 1880–1962* (South Bend, Ind.: University of Notre Dame, 1963), p. 260.

34. Author's Interview with Dr. Salvador Allende, October 14, 1965.

35. For an example of Christian Democratic neo-Thomism, see Jacques Chonchol and Julio Silva Solar, *Hacia un Mundo Comunitario: Condiciones de una Politica Social Cristiana* (Santiago: Editorial Universitaria, 1961).

36. Gil, *The Political System*, p. 66.

37. See Ernest Halperin, *Nationalism and Communism in Chile* (Cambridge, Mass.: M.I.T. Press, 1965).

38. Gil, *The Political System*, pp. 299–301.

39. *Jorge Ivan Hubner Gallo*, "Catholic Social Justice, Authoritarianism and Class Stratification," *The Conflict between Church and State in Latin America*, ed, Frederick B. Pike (New York: Alfred A. Knopf, 1964), pp. 197–207.

40. Ibid., p. 199.

41. Ibid., p. 206.

42. Ibid., p. 207.

43. Eduardo Frei Montalvo, "Catholic Social Justice, Democracy and Pluralism," in *The Conflict between Church and State*, pp. 208–17.

44. Ibid., p. 208.

45. Ibid., p. 213.

46. Gil, *The Political System*, p. 270.

47. Frei Montalvo, "Catholic Social Justice," p. 215.

48. Ibid.

49. Ibid.

50. Moreno, *Legitimacy and Stability*, p. 169.

51. Petras, *Politics and Social Forces*, p. 258.

52. Ibid., p. 257.

53. This is based on many conversations this author has had with young Christian Democratic leaders.

54. *Programa Basico de Gobierno de la Unidad Popular.*

55. V. I. Lenin, *The State and Revolution* (Moscow: Foreign Languages Publishing House, N.D.), p. 9.

56. See Gil, *The Political System*, chap. 6, pp. 244–97 for a rundown of the party system prior to 1966.

6
Cuba: Assault on a "Medieval Fortress"

As in every revolution that is a revolution (e.g., the French, Soviet, and Chinese revolutions), the Cuban revolution is ultimately a war of values in that its final task is the creation of a new consciousness. What existed before the revolution serves as the raw material for what is to be. And that which is to be will be very different from what is. Cuban culture had a pattern of values which were by themselves fine equipment for the preservation of the status quo and yet served the needs of violent revolution. However, what allowed for the use of violence is that which the violence was meant to destroy. It would be very valuable at this point to examine the interesting marriage within Cuba of ordering Thomism and the legacy of centuries of violence in Spain and the New World. For it is this combination of values with which the Cuban revolutionaries took power and against which the most progressive of them struggle. However, this bitter struggle will have to be waged with much introspection and much self-criticism, for this new value system can be a vehicle of delusion and lead those who feel they are in command back to the worst abuses of the system they attempted to destroy.

The Tradition of the Savior-Leader

The Latin-Catholic cultural contest and the oppressive conditions of Batista's Cuba necessarily resulted in a rebellion which gave transcendental importance to its leader. This leader is not done justice by the term "charismatic." He must be a savior. In Latin-Catholic society, salvation (which is not a vague or unconscious goal) is not an individual possibility. One cannot and is not expected to marshall that which is positive and righteous within oneself to achieve individualized immortal redemption. The individual, as we have implied before, is not the primary focus—society, as a reflection of universal order, is. Therefore, man must live in the best possible society in order to live the best possible life. This society does not come about through the agreement of good men. It must be authorized by an ultimate source acting through its earthly representative. For 300 years the Spanish king was the fountainhead of the Spanish earthly order. The removal of the Spanish king by Napoleon introduced an age of instability and corrupt and violent attempts to fill the vacant throne.

Relative and temporary stability had been achieved in some Latin countries almost always through force—*caudillismo* or army rule. Although Cuba had known such force and the *caudillismo* of Machado and Batista, its short life had not provided liberation from instability, corruption, and violent attempts to fill a power vacuum. Perhaps further discussion will reveal some of the reasons for this particular failing. Consistent with the view that the society of man is beset by mortal imperfections and salvation must be imposed by divine inspiration or an act of transcendency, Eduardo Chibas, a frustrated reformer and leader of the Orthodox Party, committed suicide during his radio program in 1951. This act of martyrdom, an attempt to confirm the transcendent act as the inspiration necessary to align society with the vision of the heavenly city, provided in part the series of events and the inspiration which brought a new savior to Cuba.

Chibas's death shocked and unified enough Cubans to threaten to elect Roberto Agramonte, an *Ortodoxo,* in 1952. It was against the threat of this government that Fulgencio Batista moved to establish his corrupt seven-year dictatorship. Fidel Castro was an *Ortodoxo* and a follower of the popular reform line of Chibas and, confronted with the unholy activity of Batista and the legacy of the martyr Chibas, Castro cast himself in the role of the Cuban savior. It is with this role that Castro has to struggle. He must at once inspire and rationalize the Cuban revolution. This dilemma of the revolution was created by the existence of the savior role in Cuban history.

Fidel Castro, by his appearance and his activity, conforms to these role expectations. For he is more than charismatic and more significant than the many *caudillos* who have led Latin societies since the fall of the Spanish Empire. He combines the simple yet charismatic effect of the savior with the order conceived of by St. Thomas. He embodies at once force and austerity. His uniform symbolizes simplicity, militancy, and sacrifice. His beard is a Latin Catholic sign of the vow, not to be removed until the fulfillment of prayer. He occupies no *presidencia.* He is in Havana today and among the *campesinos* tomorrow. He walks among them followed by his apostolic retinue. He can be touched and seen by the simple people. He can grant absolution and mete out justice. He speaks wisely in simple language and provides courage. He is the personal symbol of the society he has helped to create. This last facet of this leadership, social origination, combines personalism with profound structure. Fidel is the Cuban revolution. The Cuban revolution is a new society. That which was has been largely swept away. But despite the unstructured style of the *jefe*'s life, every facet of the new society is organized. With the leader as example, every Cuban is asked to fill a profoundly articulating social role.

Thus, what has happened in Cuban society perpetuates the domination of the single leader, fulfills the transcendental quality of that leadership, and approaches the imposition of a complex ideal society reflecting the promise contained in the external norm. Although these are the reflections of old longings and have contributed to the origin of a revolution, the realization of a revolution as something new will require a careful departure from these sets of potentialities. If this departure is not taken, Cuba could stultify and emerge a personalist monolithic state.

The Cuban Legacy of Violence

Another revolutionary potentiality which must be reshaped and rechanneled but which was very much part of the Cuban legacy was the propensity towards violence, especially revolutionary violence. Cuban history relates violent struggles for political power. This series of conflicts began in 1868, when Carlos Manuel de Cespedes read a declaration of independence from Spain known as the *Grito de Yara*. That struggle for independence and the belief in violent solutions to political problems pervade the rest of the nineteenth century and more than half of the twentieth century. Castro's entry into Havana in January of 1959 can be seen as the culmination of the struggle for independence. Although history chronicles violence, it does not fully explain what sustained and perpetuated it as the primary tool of political action. There are a number of structural-ideological answers to the question, "Why violence?" These "answers" will be here presented not necessarily in the order of their importance but in such a way as to indicate the web of frustration for Cubans whose religious context taught them always to aspire to the divinely perfect. That which makes Cubans violent holds for all Latin Americans. That which brought about the specific Cuban revolution will be conjectured about after these preconditions are set out.

Pyramidal Structure of Cuban Society

Cuban society, like all Latin societies, has been rather pyramidal in its organization. I say "rather" in that there were perhaps a few elite groups at the top who were forced to compete with each other for the political and economic prizes available. It is trivial to separate these elites from each other in a pretense of pluralism. For all the elite groups—the military, the owners of property, the merchants, the gangsters, the *politicos*—shared in lesser or greater degree what there was to be shared. The great conflicts emerged over the degree of greed motivating each group. From an economic and social point of view, the status quo ante favored them all and denied to the vast majority of Cubans all but a vaguely longed-for share of society's rewards.

What was true for political power was valid for economic power and prestige as well. A few monopolized (in the most jealous way) whatever could be wrung from Cuban society such as it was. Further division of rewards required violence. It should never be forgotten that Cuba's elite structure was always protected by a powerful foreign force. When Spain was ejected as the external prop, the United States quickly replaced her. That the uneven polarization of Cuban society was protected by a superior foreign power compounded the frustration of the few who were unenfranchised yet politically conscious. The root of the problem was truly transcendental and certainly colossal. It would take a transcendental (and violence is that, when looked at as a political device) and colossal effort to destroy or even rearrange the pyramid.

Those who were at the top of the social pyramid and benefitting from its existence rationalized the situation in a way that could only be contradicted by violence. If God justifies your position, you yourself do not have the right to change things. The counter to righteousness is violent contradiction. Better dead than a heretic, especially if heresy means surrendering one's God-given station. Besides, a narrow elite structure means a narrow monopoly of the equipment of violence. The easiest response to challenge is to obliterate it. Violence saves conservation and preserves energy for what is needed most. Manipulate your equals if you can, but certainly crush those below who challenge.

In essence, Cuba's experience before Castro was, as Irving Louis Horowitz has stated it, "institutionalized illegitimacy."[1] That is to say, power rested neither in law nor as a function of wider popular participation. It was narrow in scope, passing back and forth among few challengers and always unequally shared with the United States. Succession as a peaceful process was never achieved in that the processes of authoritative decision-making were seen as the cynical channels of gross exploitation. A dualism most likely existed in the minds of the temporary incumbents and certainly in the minds of those challenging the incumbents. On the one hand, if one were politicized in a Catholic context, power itself would seem the legitimizing agent. On the other hand, everywhere along the elite line, challenges existed to the exercise of that power. And no one leader could scan the people and feel comfortable in their approval. Fear, cynicism, apathy, and disapproval all were properties of the Cuban population. In summary, no Cuban ruling group since the Proclamation of the Republic in 1902 ever exercized sovereignty. The real sovereign was the United States. Therefore, those who ruled did so with the insecurity that breeds violently reacting paranoia. Those who were out of office sought power in the context of frustration which again prompts violence. The Cuban political situation was in effect one where an insecurely aspiring Thomist practiced Macchiavelli to convince himself of his own legitimacy.

The Political System

Another inducement to violence was the fierce ideological setting of the political arena. Fear on the one side and frustration on the other, as well as the dismal state of things, produced many "true solutions," documents and purveyors of truth who recognized heresy in contradiction. Again there emerges the universal Latin appeal of total ideologies that promise total solutions. From 1933 until 1952 totalism meant that in the name of one truth or another or one group or another, the central government should so augment its strength as to be able to (1) control the fiercely competing interest groups and (2) actually solve Cuba's problems. The political spectrum contained Falangists who admired the *Justicialismo* of Juan Perón; Communists under the banner of the Popular Socialist Party; reformers such as the *Autenticos,* an *APRISTA* party, who felt that the application of the liberal constitution of 1940 would provide the needed solution; *Ortodoxos,* led by Eduardo Chibas, who claimed to be orthodox *Autenticos;* and conservatives whose party names reflect nineteenth-century democratic panaceas, such as Democratic, Republican, and Liberal parties. In most cases, the ideological appeal of each of the parties was personified in the charisma of the party leader. Thus the god-head of Cuban salvation consisted of both ideology and person. A type of mystical reciprocity existed. The truth qua ideology expressed itself through a man and the man embodied and expressed the ideology. This personification credited the incumbent leader with both more power than he actually possessed and more vulnerability than a non-charismatic leader would have had. Sweep away the incumbent, thereby negate his ideology, and replace both with your own all-powerful combination of leader-ideology.

In essence, for those Cubans who sought power, thought about power, were subjected to and exercised political power, the political system was not an alien political morass. It was instead a living, responsible entity. Cubans knew whom to blame. They knew that sweeping away the culpable by whatever means necessary would bring solutions. In fact, two villains were always extant and always targets. One was the current leader, the other, the United States, who bolstered that leader. The leader also recognized his enemies. They were everyone not in power. Those he could not buy he had to consider exiling or eliminating.

However, no matter how much the charismatic leader promised as an ideal (that is, when he was out of power), reality always contradicted that promise. Chibas had to die to form a constituency. Grau San Martin, the *Autentico,* was not quite the administrator necessary to manipulate the cumbersome and corrupt political system. Batista was undereducated and used power too negatively to unite Cuba. His reign was repressive, but somehow not comprehensive. There was much room for opposition. In that he was violent, Cubans knew well how to oppose him violently. Those would-be saviors all failed to divest Cuba of foreign domination. In fact, their leadership was always so insecure, in effect, so imperfect, that their continuance in power seemed hypocrisy. For in Cuba as in all of Latin America, the leader is omnipotent or impotent; and this is another inducement to violence. Omnipotence, which is as much a function of style and legality as of force, satisfies the Latin longing for totalism. When it exists, it convinces the Latin that the omnipotent leader is divinely sanctioned. When the leader is as patently ineffective as those who attempted to rule before Castro, it is practically a duty to sweep him away.

Thus, until Castro descended from the Sierra, reality's defeat of the ideal inspired a restless and violent pursuit of that ideal. If any power less than the ideal could have served to calm the unresolved nature of Cuban reality, violence would not have been required. This dichotomous interpretation of power, omnipotence or impotence, perfection or intolerable imperfection, was another waiting snare for the Castro revolution. Castro has survived serious mistakes and failures partly because his forth-right self-criticism at once defied the ideal of the perfect leader and demonstrated the security of his power. The challenge to the ideal will be discussed more fully later. It is enough to list it as a factor in allowing the revolution and at the same time threatening it.

Scholasticism and Emotion

Violence is also a consequence of the Cuban rejection of empirical reason and exaltation of scholasticism and emotion. The history of Cuban letters depicts an early emphasis on Thomistic philosophy and Aristotelian logic with a later shift to positivism and romanticism. Life is reflected upon either with great detached cerebration or emotionally in a way that is aimed at exhorting the Cuban people to recognize their greatness.

> We Cubans are few in number, but we are illustrious. Our history is not just history, it is an epic. Nothing that we do is mere fact, it is a doughty deed, a fiery feat. Except for our stature, everything about us is great and admirable.[2]

John Gillin has characterized Cuban thought as follows:

> The word is valued more highly than the thing. The manipulation of symbols . . . is more cultivated than the manipulation of natural forces and objects. Patterns of medieval and sixteenth century mysticism are strong . . . and these patterns show no inconsistency with those of argumentation, for, as with the medieval scholastics, the worth of the logic lies in the manipulation of concepts, not in the empirical investigation of premises.[3]

Interestingly enough, most of Cuba's men of letters, whatever fields of knowledge they explored, were first of all poets, appealing to the hearts of others or later involved with morbid introspection. This is not an attempt to denigrate poetry, poets, or metaphysics. However, it is an attempt to show the otherworldly, introspective, if you will, egoistic, nature of prerevolutionary thought. Life could never be dealt with as it existed. It was idealized or unconsidered. It was unified and totalized, rarely analyzed. Here again, as in Mexico, we recognize the culture of oppression and Fanon's psychology of "avoidance." By escaping into the ego and the abstract, the intellectual avoided confronting the real and powerful forces that threatened his sense of self. In such a context, mundane human life was of little value. Martí, so many years in exile, a diligent worker for independence and a prolific writer, had to die a dramatic death before he achieved the transcendence necessary for him to be appreciated. Then he became *El Apóstol,* the apostle, spreading the gospel of the most transcendent of Cuban realities, glorious independence.

When men must die before they achieve grace, then human life must be viewed as an encumbrance. If the ideal is to be achieved, then life must be sacrificed. Politics as a game of talk, manipulation, and compromise is a tiresome task with at best a cynical goal. Real achievement (that is, ideal achievement) can only be gained through dramatic death-dealing struggle. Since the ideal, the exclusively cerebral and/or emotional goal, can never be achieved without destroying it in its concrete existence, the struggle must continue. Violence is the baptism of grace in this struggle in that it confers beatifying death.

The relationship between romantic idealism and violence has intruded itself into the current Cuban revolution and was the context for the initiation of that revolution. However, to conclude that this romantic idealism is a subversive force in Cuba would be too simplistic and certainly too strong a dose of ethnocentric myopia. North Americans are taught to value narrow, mechanical pragmatism which respects efficiency and distrusts abstractions. Pragmatism encourages people to get the job done without developing the ideological vision to ask why or for whom. Cuba dares to transcend the quicksand of mundane reality. The real danger of this particular Cuban romantic idealism comes from the scholastic legacy of this romantic outgrowth. It will be shown later how easily seduced is the Thomist totalizer by the totalizing quality of Marxism. The danger involved in this seduction is that Marxism becomes dogmatic and evolves into the cerebral detachment of scholasticism. Within this heady context, the revolutionary's romantic ideals might be as applicable to the canals of Mars as the shores of the Caribbean. There is the additional danger that revolutionaries will build a scholastic wall between themselves and sources of practical criticism. This romantic idealism, a legacy of sterile scholasticism (and a later highly illusory positivism, which itself articulated well with the apolitical ideal of Thomism), could lure the leadership into disastrous unreality. Cuba's first experience with such a possibility was the wholesale purchase of the idea of industrialization as the necessary first step toward the building of socialism. This dogmatic but impractical move was adopted from the Soviet model; however, the Soviet Union never pushed the model itself. Although the error of this line was quickly appreciated, some, like K. S. Karol, feel that the attempt to produce 10 million tons of sugar in 1970 was an equally reckless example of pursuing absolutes. I will evaluate the "Year of the Heroic Effort" later in this chapter.

A New Future from the Past

Cuba's past has obviously formed Cuba's future. It is also obvious that this past must be constantly criticized, evaluated, and dealt with as it appears in the ideas and behavior of the Cuban people, both leaders and masses. This struggle to overcome, synthesize, and construct a new future out of the past will be partially chronicled below. It is this struggle which differentiates Cuba from Mexico and from an earlier Chile.

The Cuban revolution is involved in a struggle for the minds of the people, while the Mexican revolution never involved the majority of the population in this type of struggle, and Chile is just beginning to approach this problem, which signifies some basic differences among these three Latin nations. Cuba is a large island in well-traveled waters. She had long been exposed to constant economic and intellectual penetration from the United States and Great Britain.

Cuba's Indians and their culture were destroyed in the first hundred years of Spanish domination. Therefore, Cuban society was not built in the foundations of great pre-Columbian civilizations. There is no great pre-Columbian legacy or longing among Cuba's masses.

Although Cuba's large African population did synthesize its music, religion, and language on the island, this African culture came to Cuba in fragments, not as a totality as did the folkways and *ejidos* of Mexico.

Socialist Political Culture

The Cuban economy has always been a plantation economy. After the Indian labor force was destroyed, Cuba used African slaves. When slavery was abolished, wage labor was substituted. And Cuban labor was not socialized by the feudal type relations of the Chilean *fundo* or the Mexican *hacienda*. According to Maurice Zeitlin and James O'Connor, the Cuban revolution in its inception, unlike the Mexican struggle, had major Marxist characteristics. Zeitlin's argument is extremely interesting in that it differentiates the Cuban revolution not only from other Latin revolutions, but from other socialist revolutions. He writes:

> My leading hypothesis is: Cuba is the first socialist revolution to take place in a capitalist country—a country in which the owning class was capitalist and the direct producers were wage workers.[4]

Two conclusions drawn from Zeitlin's argument are extremely important in differentiating the Cuban experience from those of Mexico and Chile and explaining the possibilities of building a new consciousness in Cuba. The first conclusion is that the Cuban revolution began with a potentially unified labor force in the context of an integrated economy and socialized both in the agrarian and urban sectors alike by capitalist relations of production. This helps us to understand how the Cuban revolution has been able to meet the requirements of socialist integration. In the stage of guerrilla warfare, fighters from the city had to integrate their struggle with that of agrarian workers in their mutual dependence on the countryside. This first phase set the stage for the physical and psychological integration of the socialist society.

The second conclusion, based on Zeitlin's interviews with workers, was that

> . . . there was in the working class of Cuba a socialist political culture (of anarcho-syndicalist and communist elements) born in an insurrectionary past, which had already existed for no less than three decades (and for longer in segments such as the tobacco workers). The outlook of the typical worker toward the system was impregnated by socialist ideas; what is most important, the vision of a future without capitalism was most firmly and widely held by the most decisive sectors of the working class.[5]

This socialist political culture did not grow spontaneously out of capitalist relations of production. A peculiarly unjust wage-labor system and high under-employment and unemployment did make workers particularly receptive to the clandestine and open propaganda of Cuba's Communists. Zeitlin tells of the importance of this socialist mentality among the Cuban labor force:

> When the Revolutionary Government was established, it had a mass-class base that likely was beyond its leaders in its vision of the society to be created by the revolution. This is in striking contrast to the situation in other countries in which the revolutionary leaders were far beyond their own mass base. The fact of a socialist political culture in

the working class—a nationally-based, cohesive working class—combined with the force of nationalism and anti-imperialism, created a potent revolutionary force waiting to be tapped by the revolutionary leaders once they took power.[6]

Although these socialist workers certainly did form a vanguard element and did point the way to socialism once the revolution took power, it would be erroneous to believe that the marriage of a socialist labor force and a socialist revolutionary leadership would automatically negate the impact of nearly 400 years of Spanish imperialism and the dramatic influence of a half-century of American-dominated capitalist development.

First, although Zeitlin emphasizes the importance of this socialist work force, Cuba, like Mexico and Chile, is an underdeveloped or at least a semi-developed country. One of the characteristics of contemporary underdevelopment pointed out by Castro himself is that a relatively small percentage of the population is in the work force. As late as 1970, with full employment, Castro states that only 32% of the population is of age to participate in production. The rest of the population is either too young or too old to engage in production. Furthermore, Castro points out that of this 32%, a fair percentage are in the military and in social services and therefore not in production.[7]

Second, socialism requires the integration of theory and practice, i.e., a socialist mentality is only half formed if it is not informed by socialist practice. It should be remembered that the socializing context of the Cuban work force and therefore its practice was capitalistic in an atavistic Latin Catholic value context. That prior conditions did not automatically produce a developed and efficient socialism in Cuba will be seen later when Castro's and Guevara's criticism of their own revolution are studied.

Anti-imperialism in Cuba

Another difference between the Cuban experience and that of Mexico or Chile is that imperialism has never been hidden in Cuba. The resources and ultimate control of the island have always been in the hands of foreigners. Since 1868, Cuba's revolutionary struggle was always waged against the imperialists as principal enemies. Although that nineteenth-century enemy was ostensibly Spain, Cuba had already been heavily penetrated by North American capital. One of Spain's major functions was to keep Cuba stable in order to provide a healthy climate for the prosperity of foreign investment. On the eve of the first Pan-American Conference in 1889, Martí warned the Latin nations to unite against North American imperialism. "Spanish America succeeded in overcoming the tyranny of Spain, and now, after examining the background causes and factors of the invitation to the

Washington conference with a judicial eye, it is urgent to say—for it is the truth—that the hour has come for Spanish America to declare her second independence."[8]

Although Castro's 1953 *History Will Absolve Me* is not a direct attack on the United States, its references to foreign domination of parts of the Cuban economy make it obvious that Castro was aware of the necessity for a struggle against Batista and imperialism.

> Eighty-five percent of the small farmers in Cuba pay rent and live under the constant threat of being dispossessed from the land they cultivate. More than half the best cultivated land belongs to foreigners. In Oriente, the largest province, the lands of the United Fruit Company and West Indian Company join the north coast to the southern one. There are two hundred thousand peasant families who do not have a single acre of land to cultivate to provide food for their starving children. On the other hand, nearly three hundred thousand *caballerias* of productive land owned by powerful interests remains uncultivated.[9]

From these statements we can see the anti-imperialist content of Cuban revolutionary thought. The anti-imperialist current of the revolution has been a major factor of the development of a society which rejects both the imperialist and the lifeway of the people of the imperialist nation.

Chilean and Mexican leaders have also been conscious of imperialism. However, both these nations rid themselves of Spain early in the nineteenth century. They both therefore have had at least the appearance and the custom of independence. In addition, the size of one nation and the distance of the other nation from the United States have made for a qualitative difference in their struggle for self-determination. The anti-imperialist thread of the Cuban revolution will be picked up later in the discussion of Cuban education.

The Middle Class

It should not be forgotten that although Fidel Castro is of the middle class, the revolution he has led is not a middle-class phenomenon. Castro is a true rebel. He has rebelled against his class. He did not choose to lead the people by accident as did Padre Hidalgo. He did not lead a revolution merely to bring political reforms as did Madero. Neither did he win political office through a bourgeois democratic political process as Allende did in Chile.

As was pointed out in the chapter on Mexico, Fidel's central focus has been justice for the masses. It should be pointed out that, contrary to popular understanding, Castro not only pledged himself to the masses, but the majority of those who followed him into battle at Moncada and into the Sierra Maestra were of the popular classes. Hugh Thomas points out that of the 168 who actually made the assault on Moncada, only 9 beside Castro himself appear to have had any higher education. In fact, the major class in both actions was proletarian.[10]

It is sometimes pointed out, presumably to denigrate the importance of the Sierra Maestra campaign and therefore to elevate the importance of the middle-class resistance to Batista, that the guerrillas never had a force much larger than 300 men fighting in the mountains. To stop at this figure is to misunderstand the nature and necessity of guerrilla warfare and truly to begin to misunderstand the thrust and purposes of the revolution. The guerrillas did not pin down the main body of Batista's forces as 300 isolated fighters. The guerrillas were successful only in as much as the peasantry supported them. It was peasants who brought the disunited and disoriented rebels together after the debacle at Belic. It was the peasantry who supplied food, sometimes shelter, guides, informants, and intelligence networks for the rebel forces. The peasantry also welded the countryside to the city by joining ranks with the originally urban fighters. This is said not to discredit the role middle-class revolutionaries played in both withdrawing support from Batista, lending support to the guerrillas in the Sierra Maestra, and directly attacking the *caudillo* as did the Student Directorate in Havana. But the truth is that the Cuban middle class had discredited itself as a leadership group after the ratification of the American-dictated Constitution of 1902 and after fifty-seven years of corruption and complete dependence on the United States. This dependence, so well perpetuating and so well perpetuated by the North American stranglehold on the economy, disallowed the Cuban middle sector from ever becoming a class in and for itself.

The bankruptcy of this class was evident to Castro soon after the seizure of power in Havana in 1959. It will be remembered that Castro made an attempt to step to the rear and to place in the forefront of the revolution an impeccably honest and patriotically middle-class government. Although this government had Castro's seal, it could not rule. Human history has shown that chaotic times require strong leaders, i.e., leaders who are strong because their own unique and decisive characteristics coincide with the needs and expectations of the people they are to lead. There are those who believe that Latin societies will live in chaos unless they have strong leadership. Within the Catholic value structure, the reverence for absolutes is brought to mind. The leader has all power or none at all.

Cuba in the early days of 1959 was chaotic enough. The *cuadillo* of seven years had left. Castro had come down from the Sierra, the obvious focus of a leaderless people. Yet he was not to be found among the honest but pallid group of middle-class men who merely repeated the contradiction of middle-class "leadership" in Cuba. Their leadership confirmed their dependency. Herbert Matthews quotes Manuel Urrutia, the man Castro placed in the presidency:

> Perhaps no man has ever reached the Presidency under circum-
> stances more difficult than mine. I had only nominal power; all real

power, political and military, was in the hands of Fidel Castro. He was supported not only by his personal prestige but by his revolutionary organization, by the Rebel Army and by popular fervor. Nevertheless, I was ready to collaborate loyally with the Revolution and with Fidel Castro in accomplishing everything he had pledged to the people.[11]

However, Urrutia's protestations of loyalty to the contrary, this middle-class gentleman did not seem ready to go along with the radical tide of revolution. Matthews relates the information of Lopez-Fresquet, himself one of those first middle-class Cabinet ministers, that Urrutia was sabotaging the revolution. Lopez-Fresquet claimed that, for one thing, Urrutia delayed signing bills. "His conduct disrupted the functioning of government."[12] Urrutia and the middle class had neither legitimacy nor the ability to shake loose the cynically self-interested middle-class vision of a revolution as a series of institutional reforms. As it was with Madero in Mexico, their vision cut them off from the needs of the people.

In contrasting the failure of the Cuban middle class with the success of their Mexican counterparts, one is struck by differences in history, social organization, relations of production, and the strengths and weaknesses of the lower classes.

The Mexican middle class was also corrupt and beholden through much of history to foreign support. However, Mexico had at least the veneer of independence. Many bloody struggles were fought in the name of this independence. It was the *criollos* in league with the Church and the oligarchs who had ridden Mexico of Spain. The middle class and those who soon assumed middle-class roles expelled the pseudo-empire of Maximillian and Carlota. The fact that the majority of Mexicans languished in poverty and oppression under middle-class domination was not enough to make that domination intolerable. Mexico of 1910 was not Cuba of the 1950s. It was a basically agrarian country whose *campesinos* lived on feudal *haciendas*. The peasant leaders never seemed able to transcend the provincial boundaries of their feudal-Catholic-Indian perspective. Although they were willing to deny loyalty to and rebel against the middle class in Mexico City, the stakes for which they fought seemed consistently to be limited to peasant control of a static, non-integrated countryside. Unlike the wage laborer and small holder *guajiros* of Cuba, they had no broad-visioned leader and no urban proletariat of consequence to join with them and lead them for each others' benefit.

The Chilean middle sector differs from the Cuban middle class in that it was never terribly corrupt in the normal sense of the word, nor has it been discredited in the eyes of the people. The upper ranges of the middle class were soon incorporated into the oligarchy, placing a stranglehold on the national economy by a fairly united class. Although economic imperialism is an important factor in the undermining of the Chilean economy, this fact was obscured by Chile's distance from the United States and by the formula for legitimacy institutionalized by Portales in the 1830s. The institutional mechanism has been broad enough and flexible enough to channel and co-opt dissent, always led by the middle class. The Chilean bourgeois-democratic state has been what its name implies. It has been a sophisticated mechanism built by the middle class for use through middle-class skills. It has for so many years mediated the antagonisms of one class while using the electoral and disruptive potential of the lower classes as a weapon in its own struggle. It is not strange that today in Chile, the triumph of the peasants and workers is led by men of the middle class socialized by bourgeois-democratic politics.

These differences in the character and past of the middle class in three countries struggling with history perhaps underline Cuba's need to build totally new leadership, and on the model of that leadership, a new man. The old was either corrupt or tainted and broken by oppression and exploitation. The old leadership and its class, faced with its bankruptcy, its inability to seize the chance to lead, has exiled itself in great numbers. Leadership rebounds on those who struggled most against the old.

The Role of the Church

The Church was never as powerful in Cuba as it was in Mexico nor even as it has been in Chile. Perhaps for that reason the Cuban Church has not been heavily attacked under socialism.

The Church's weakness in Cuba stemmed from the fact that Cuba was not worth a large investment of personnel, given the paucity of the Indian population. Catholicism with its very structured view of the universe has always been more at home relating to the communal entirety of Indian societies than with the fragmented relationships of slave society. In that Cuba's Indian population was annihilated at about the same time that Mexico was opened up, the natural investment for the Church was in the rich, highly structured civilizations of Indian Mexico.

This is not to discount the coincidence of a large, intact Indian population with the existence of great mineral and land wealth whose possession was concomitant with political power in the empire.

That Cuba had neither proselytizing possibilities nor relative wealth diminished the Church's institutional importance, but it did not erase the fact that those who ruled were Catholic. And those who ruled lived almost exclusively until the triumph of the revolution—in Havana. The implication of this demographic fact is that although the Church was unable to dominate the Cuban countryside completely, this did not radically diminish the Church's influence in the ruling city. Thus, although the island was pounded by many intellectual currents, the philosophical struggles were always in the context of and mostly against a Catholic world outlook. This is why today the struggle to build a new society and thus a new man must be fought against three enemies. One is the capitalist atavisms of the old society. Second is the absolutistic scholasticism, fatalism, and hierarchical tendencies of the Catholic value context. The third is the pitfall of elitism and bureaucratism which socialist organization can so easily carry forward from dependent capitalism.

It is the struggle against these enemies plus the strong desire of the Cuban leaders to move forward to a new society which has prompted the revolutionaries to make of society a school in which one learns, and participates as one produces. The ideal, of course, is to give man's production back to him in the form of visible social advance.

The Task of Achieving
Distributive Justice

This struggle has always had fantastically difficult contradictions obstructing its path. The revolution's first task was to achieve, as rapidly as possible, enough distributive justice to convince the population that it was indeed involved in a revolution, not just another seizure of power. In that the economic thrust of the revolution was rapid and penetrating, the people were convinced. As a result, the majority of the population was enthusiastic and ready for revolutionary mobilization. However, another majority, a majority of Cuba's middle sectors, those who finally had the technical skills to contribute to the creation of new wealth, left the country disgruntled and disenchanted. It would be incorrect to feel that Cuba's prerevolutionary middle sectors could have provided anything near the kind, and quality of knowledge and resources Cuba needed to move into revolutionary development. Cuba under imperialist domination did not develop and did not need the number of technicians she needed as an independent and developing socialist country. But the old educated groups might have provided at least a training base to develop new personnel.

Another immediate contradiction in the struggle to serve a neglected population was that the social service needs of the country were and remain so great that the educated people who did stay were greedily snatched up into these nonproductive sectors of the economy. In 1971, one-third of the 32% of the population engaged in activities related to the economy were public health, education, and defense workers. The 32% figure itself presents a big problem to the advance of the revolution. For when the Cuban economy was organized to serve the people, it was found that the nonproductive young and old would continue to burden the small work force and the limited wealth of an underdeveloped country. This shortage will not be overcome, given current population figures, until at least 1980.

The Struggle to Form a Party

If the raw statistics of deficiency and drain were contradictory to Cuba's leap forward, so certainly was her socialist organizing ability. It must be kept in mind at all times in viewing Cuba that her stated goal is not only to develop, but to develop socialist man. This double task is doubly difficult. Not only must Cuba produce commodities, create new material wealth, and train a population to participate as efficient elements in the system of production, but production must emerge as an equal and integral part of the development of a socialist consciousness. In essence, Cuba is not only producing to produce; she produces to educate as well. To accomplish this task, she needed an organized cadre of a very high level of socialist consciousness. People were needed who were theoretically sophisticated and could organize an underdeveloped people to learn and work. Most important, this cadre would establish and maintain the vital relationship between vanguard and masses which keeps socialism alive and developing.

Although Castro recognized himself as a Marxist-Leninist leader early in the revolution, he also recognized the limitations of the "unsophisticated" guerrilla leadership in its ability to fulfill this complex role. The shortcomings of the *foco* method of revolutionary insurrection were probably evident to Castro as he first reached for the militants of the old P.S.P. *(Partido Socialista Popular,* the Cuban Communist Party) to fulfill the key organizing role.[13] The rebellion in the Sierra Maestra had not been conducted by a group of self-conscious, studying Marxists. The men of the Sierra were a mixed class group of liberal humanists. Little theory informed their practice. That their practice was repetitive of Maoist guerrilla experience was discovered by the rebels after their own experience had already shaped their method. When Fidel proclaimed to himself, to Cuba, and to the world that he was a Marxist-Leninist, he was declaring his understanding of events past and future, not confirming the deliberate design of past practices. The Twenty-sixth of July revolutionaries and the P.S.P. militants presented Cuba with practice without theory and theory without practice, respectively.

Role of the P.S.P. in Cuba

This description of the P.S.P. might be contested, however. The *Partido Socialista Popular* sprang from the organizational thrust of the Third International and the establishment of the Comintern. It was established in 1925, and it should be remembered that Cuba received its first constitution only twenty-three years previously and its "independence" only twenty-seven years before these events in socialist history. The party had participated in all the political and social turmoil that had characterized the island's history up to and including the fall of Batista. However, although the party (like all Communist parties) conceives of itself as a vanguard organization, its true role was more educational than immediately political. As was stated above, the Communists did a good job in clandestinely preparing a portion of Cuba's workers for socialism. But in such major events as the rebellion against Machado, the attack on Moncada, and the rebellion in the Sierra, the party found itself much less than a vanguard. As has been the case with Communist parties throughout Latin America, the Cuban party found itself in constant fear of "adventurism" and in constant distrust of the people. K. S. Karol claims that the P.S.P.'s "congenital fault was that it tried to transfer into the neo-colonial situation of Cuba, an underdeveloped country, the precise revolutionary scheme its comrades had developed for the capitalist countries of Europe."[14] Within this illusory concept of their country's major contradictions, the party ignored American domination and all those other forces not in labor who struggled against Machado. This was true even though the labor force constituted little more than 16% of the economically active population. The party thus initiated its activity in a dogmatic bind. It dismissed as petit-bourgeois-anarchist a long tradition of anti-imperialist struggle. Its catechism was printed in Stalin's Soviet Union and swallowed whole, unquestioned by the party members.

It has been pointed out that Fidel Castro follows in a line of brilliant and daring Cuban revolutionaries. K. S. Karol cites the stories of two of these predecessors, Julio Antonio Mello and Ruben Martinez Villena. Both of these men were Communists, both were inspiring in their assaults on tyranny and their leadership and organizational ability. Both died young and both had difficulties with the party. The party required selfless dedication which was to manifest itself in discipline. The party thus resolved the contradiction between control and daring in favor of control and found itself commenting on but not leading the daring expeditions which eventually put socialism in power. When the party did move, as in August of 1933 in the leadership of the Transport Workers Central Strike Committee, they found themselves much less militant than the transport workers, who had struck to destroy the Machado regime. The party understood the strike they ostensibly led to be based on the desire for pay raises. When the party was ready to settle and therefore betray potential revolution, the workers ignored the settlement and brought Machado down. This story is recounted because it typifies the gap between the P.S.P.'s dogmatic rendering of reality and the real dynamism of the Cuban revolutionary situation. Although the events and personalities just mentioned are part of the history of the twenties and thirties, the party's relation to the events of the fifties is similar. It is one thing to educate and even organize people and another thing entirely to lead them in the overthrow of the state. To do the latter, certain qualities are indispensable. One is daring; rebellion is always risky. Second is confidence in the people, which must flow from knowledge of the people and their reality. Without these qualities a revolutionary party is revolutionary in name only and will constantly be mistaken and hesitant, always lagging behind and frequently antagonizing the people.

Castro's Use of the P.S.P.

Castro's attack on Moncada was daring, if nothing else. However, as has been pointed out, daring is a very Cuban quality. It captures the imagination of Cubans because it is a confirmation of *machismo*. The assault failed to capture the fort or to ignite an uprising, but it triumphed in that it gave Castro some prominence as a daring rebel. Before, he had been another young, articulate politician, but a politician nevertheless. It also created martyrs, who certainly have their place in the Latin Catholic lexicon. The attack also defined the Cuban situation. The regime was further defamed by the stories leaking out of its prisons. Castro became a voice for all those who denounced Batista and his gangsters.

The party stood back and in turn denounced Castro for his petit-bourgeois adventurism even though they admired his daring. In fairness, it should be pointed out that the P.S.P was protecting itself in light of the failure of the attack to topple Batista. For in an era of rabid red-baiting, the party was to sustain heavy attack from the regime, even though Communists were innocent of complicity in the attack. It was not until 1958, when Batista was isolated by almost all elements of Cuban society, that the party felt the imperative to exhibit its own revolutionary colors. It was clear that they had to join the revolution behind Castro's Sierra vanguard or be isolated again.

This has not been said to denigrate Castro's choice of the P.S.P. militants to organize the real vanguard party that a socialist revolution needs. The P.S.P. militants were the only learned, disciplined, organized Marxists in Cuba. Castro quickly appreciated that to initiate a real revolution is to open oneself to necessity more than choice, at least in the beginning. The revolution demanded and Castro had to accede. The choice of the P.S.P. to give institutional structure to the revolution might have been a very positive move in transforming Cuba. There is no doubt that for a person, plan, or organization to succeed, Castro's seal of legitimacy was needed. By legitimizing the P.S.P., Castro opened the possibility of depersonalizing the revolution through his own personal power. However, the P.S.P.'s own contradictory past and dogmatism postponed the depersonalization process.

Anibal Escalante, Castro's chosen P.S.P. organizer, discounted the revolutionary experience and consciousness of anyone not of the P.S.P. This was true even though Castro felt

> . . . that the masses had become revolutionary, that the masses had embraced Marxist ideology, that the masses had embraced Marxism-

Leninism. That was an unquestionable fact. The camps had been de
fined; the enemies had declared themselves as such; the laboring masses
the peasants, the student masses, the masses of the poor, the under
privileged masses of our nation, significant portions of the middle class
sections of the petty bourgeoisie, intellectual workers, made Marxist
Leninist ideas their own, made the struggle against imperialism thei
own, made the struggle for the Socialist Revolution their own.[15]

In short, if Castro were correct, the people were ready to learn to take the
revolution into their own hands and this could only come about through the
depersonalization of the leadership process. However, according to Cas
tro's purge speech, the ever present "virus" of personalism was about to
destroy the possibility of the formation of a vanguard party. To stem the
spread of this disease, Castro was forced after a long period of apparently
quiet toleration to apply his own immense power and prestige to remove
this sectarian pretender to the throne. The O.R.I. (Integrated Revolutionary
Organization) was thus abandoned before it functioned.

Fagen claims that the Escalante blunder ended the importance of the old
P.S.P. as a semi-autonomous power within the new Marxist-Leninist organization which emerged after the O.R.I. attempt had failed. P.S.P. militants
themselves were not totally discredited but instead were submerged as a
separate vanguard group and combined with the militants produced by the
struggle for power or those who had discovered the leadership in the post-
Batista revolutionary struggle. In 1965 the new organization, P.U.R.S.C.
(United Party of the Cuban Socialist Revolution) evolved into the Communist party of Cuba. Although old P.S.P. members were laced through the
organs of the new party, they were in the minority compared to larger
numbers of previously non-Marxist revolutionaries.

Creating a New Consciousness:
Education and Revolutionary
Participation

It should not be thought that the struggle to form a vanguard party was the
only organizational front on which the battle to create a new consciousness
was fought. Fagen, in his book, *The Transformation of Political Culture in
Cuba,* discusses a number of mobilization efforts, like the literacy drive of
1961 to 1962 and the Schools of Revolutionary Instruction, which have
since been abandoned as high-priority struggles. Another effort, the Committees for the Defense of the Revolution, is still in operation and central
to the politicization of all life in Cuba.

Schools of Revolutionary Instruction

The first of these, the struggle against illiteracy, had a very dramatic impact on extremely important elements of Cuban society and on the society as a whole. The year of 1961 was designated the Year of Education. On January 1, 100,000 young people left Havana and spread through the countryside to teach people to read. The massive move of people out of Havana was in itself a revolutionary move. The typical pattern of migration in Latin America is from the countryside to the city. In Cuba, the typical *Habanero* never left the capital if he could help it. If he were middle class, he would have been more likely to travel abroad than to the next province. In addition to this Havana chauvinism and isolation, most Cuban youth, like most other Latin Catholic youth, were well-enmeshed in the net of the extended family. Only marriage or the necessity to live near the university drew them from the family hearth. Likewise the *guajiros* found it a rare day in the thirteenth month of the year when they could travel beyond their place of birth or work, if the two happened to be different. Their own family situation was as stable as economic conditions would allow. The impact of city young on *guajiro* was thus a significant revolutionary statement for both. It did not bring about magic transformation by itself. It was a beginning—a representative of the future. Taken together with the mobilizing effect of the entire revolutionary effort, the literacy campaign was a fit beginning.

The most important lesson of the Schools of Revolutionary Instruction were learned by the revolutionaries themselves. It was a lesson that upset prerevolutionary academic ideas about education as a process separate from experience. The schools were founded in 1960 to raise the educational level of revolutionaries. Their purpose was to counteract years of anti-Marxist propaganda and to train a cadre in the skills of Marxist dialectics. Fagen tells us that the schools had a rather chaotic if rapid development. The choice of staff reflected at first the sectarian, opportunistic shortcomings of the newly organized O.R.I. in that teachers were chosen more for their P.S.P. loyalty than for ability to teach and relate to the people. Students either failed entirely to comprehend the theory they were taught or learned it in an abstract, inflexible way. When the O.R.I. was purged and remolded into the P.U.R.S.C. and finally the P.C.C., the schools were also reorganized and somewhat improved, taking on the added assignments of technological training and scientific research. However, according to Fagen, the schools continued to suffer basic problems. Students and staff remained on a low level; study materials were limited to Soviet manuals which Cubans found stilted and inapplicable to their experience. After eight years, the message was clear. The only school for revolutionary instruction was the revolution itself. Study could not be separated from experience, nor could theory be learned apart from practice. The study was dull, the theory wooden, and the schools that operated completely outside of production were an economic burden.

The failure was accepted and the schools were closed. The new reality was designed to be one in which practice would inform theory. At least in this instance, scholastic unreality was conquered and another battlement of the medieval fortress was taken.

The Committees for the Defense of the Revolution

The Committees for the Defense of the Revolution were also established in 1960. They were to serve many functions, but their major role was to serve as ultimate politicizing agencies, operating where the people lived and giving them immediate opportunity for revolutionary participation. Their primary mission was to destroy the sphere of anarchy so cherished in Catholic and bourgeois societies. The existence of the committees is a revolutionary denial of the idea that one can live in society and operate privately in one's own interest, as long as one does not invade or impair the rights of others. Cubans were to be faced with the assertion that what one does, even in one's own house, does have an impact on others and in a large or small way affects their ability to contribute to the common good. The C.D.R.'s existence and practice thus extended the idea of the family by lengthening the skein of responsibility to include one's neighbors and ultimately to the whole society.

The growth and success of the C.D.R.'s indicate that these ideas were positively greeted by most Cubans. A note of cynical perspective should add that these revolutionary block committees did attract some who were motivated by opportunism and even some motivated by the possibility of vengeance against their neighborhood enemies. However, the practice of criticism and self-criticism initiated in 1962 may have helped keep these tendencies in check. This self-regulatory practice assaults another tower of the old consciousness, i.e., the ultimate privacy and inviolability of the ego, and even *machismo,* and casts these tendencies in a new perspective. The individual is divested of his vulnerability by extending the importance of his existence to group and societal concern. Although these privatistic and anti-socialist characteristics have not been erased from Cuban consciousness, the mechanisms for their transformation have been accepted by Cubans. Whether they succeed is integral to the success of the revolution itself.

Economic Tests

The severest test of this success was put by the revolutionary leadership in the "Year of the Heroic Effort." Cuba was to cut, harvest, and refine 10 million tons of sugar in an extended harvest. There is a certain irony in this, the revolution's biggest "test" and biggest "failure." Jose Martí warned against the distortions of the sugar monoculture. This dependence on sugar was symbolic of imperialist domination. The sugar economy was responsible for vast underemployment, the neglect of the rest of Cuba's rich potential, and many other inadequacies which sentenced Cuba to underdevelopment. The escape from monoculture was a primary goal of the revolution. Through 1962, under the economic guidance of Guevara, Cuba attempted to industrialize. This was done to destroy the monoculture, to create a strong modern and independent Cuba, and to reinforce and expand the proletariat whose dictatorship is the first stage of socialism and the necessary step in the evolution of communism. By 1963, industrialization had failed and economic rethinking showed Cuba a new path toward solvency and healthy socialist development. This was the path of agricultural diversification with sugar cultivation the central if not permanent core of the plan.

One of the salient reasons for the failure of the economy in its first assault on underdevelopment was labelled "a manifestation of absolute subjectivism" by Guevara.

> We are not backed by either statistics or historical experience. We have tried to act upon nature subjectively, as if our direct contact with it would accomplish what we were after, ignoring the objective experiences of other countries. When we used to say that there is no country in the world in the process of development that has a rise in revenue of 20% a year, we told ourselves that we could do it. When we tackled the problem of growth in our country, we did not investigate what we had, what we could spend and what could allow us to develop.[16]

Referring to an impossible plan to produce 12 million more pairs of shoes than Cuba had ever produced before, Guevara said:

> A viable organization was necessary first, and we had not yet achieved it. We had only worked out, superficially, the final number and the main tasks. In reality, we had neither enough cattle nor machinery for leather. The plan was a *manifestation of absolute subjectivism* [italics mine] which referred especially to numbers in order to calculate our real possibilities, impossible to realize. It was all decisions made from the top.[17]

Although this lack of realism was compounded by other problems, it still merits top billing for the economic failures of the revolution before 1963. Realism had not yet replaced the daring which did ignite the first assaults on tyranny, but which in turn had to convert its energy into discipline, hard work, and coordination with the abilities of the masses in order for the revolution to bear a new society and not remain the static residue of another seizure of power.

The "Year of the Heroic Effort"

On January 24, 1964, in the wake of Guevara's realization of the mistake of absolute subjectivism, Fidel first began discussing the sugar harvest of 1970, the 10-million-ton harvest. In spite of the extremely low figures of 1962 (4.8 million tons) and 1963 (3.8 million tons), Fidel postulated the necessity to reemphasize the centrality of sugar production and the economic benefits that would accrue from this return. Fidel had just returned from his second visit to the U.S.S.R., where he had signed a new long-term sugar agreement. Although there is reason to understand Castro's enthusiasm and optimism, one should have been immediately wary of a repetition of the sin Guevara had identified as central to Cuba's previous economic malaise. For Castro, the necessity would have to become the reality.

The necessity of this "heroic effort" was justified in that it was to act

> ... of itself as a mobilizing force, encouraging people to work harder and generating enthusiasm. This force is also needed for the development of a social conscience, since from now on the people will look upon each individual who does not bear his share of responsibility, who shirks his duty, does not bother to play his full part, as one who undermines the extraordinary possibilities of our country, one who acts against the interests of the whole nation.[18]

Thus the economic goal was to provide the possibility for a new thrust in the development of *el hombre nuevo.* In order to accomplish this phenomenal increment in sugar production, Fidel depended on three major labor supplements.

First was the mechanization of the harvest itself through the use of a much-touted, never-proven Soviet harvester. The properties of the machine were revealed to Castro by Khruschev who "has a great deal of experience in agriculture. ... He reorganized the economy and agriculture of the Ukraine after the Germans departed, which explains his extraordinary intimacy with agricultural questions and his knowledge of machines."[19] The machine was to both cut and reap. Its involvement in the harvest would seem to have been crucial.

Cuba's *machetero* force, diminished by retirement and better opportunities, was not in itself large enough to bring in the harvest. Neither could *"bracero"* labor imported from Haiti and the Dominican Republic be used in a socialist country as it was under imperialism. The only alternative to a mechanized harvest was one which employed an enormous volunteer labor force. This was the second supplement necessary for the harvest. Fidel felt that such an effort, a product of *conciencia,* would also strengthen *conciencia.*[20] Cubans would volunteer and the harvest would thus confirm as well as mobilize. This would be a fitting tribute to ten years of revolution.

Third, although the *zafra* used to last the 100 days of the Cuban winter, since 1968 it has been extended by several months. The 1970 harvest had an even longer life. It began in July 1969 and extended through the spring of 1970. (Although K. S. Karol claims the harvest was to last until the spring of 1971, Castro's July 26, 1970, speech was in part a eulogy for this moribund goal.)[21]

As it turned out, the Soviet machine failed. It was huge, heavy, and cumbersome. Its designers seem to have forgotten that sugar cane does not stand up straight and volunteer itself to be harvested as does wheat and rice. The stalk must be singled out from a tangle of leaves and other stalks to be cut just right. The volunteers did turn out, from all sectors of the economy as well as from many nations of the world. They labored through Cuba's hottest weather to cut, gather, and wash the cane. Their per capita output was low. They had to be transported, fed, housed, and paid their normal wages. Their ordinary jobs, all integral to the economic well-being of the nation, were neglected during their volunteer stints. Undoubtedly, many were aching and exhausted after the unfamiliar and arduous physical labor of the harvest. Their subsequent absenteeism meant further man-hour deprivation.

In order to handle the increased input of sugar, transport and the *centrales* (refineries) had to be beefed up and modernized. The prerevolutionary period had left Cuba with run-down and antiquated refineries. The harvest of 1969, which ran between 4 and 5 million tons, was processed by an infrastructure that could not easily double its capacity. Again, scarce resources had to be diverted into technological improvement and expansion. Transport too had to be channeled from its normal duties into carrying volunteers in and sugar out.

Finally, the "Heroic Effort" failed to produce 10 million tons of harvested sugar. The total was a considerable 8.5 million tons, a record harvest in itself. All in all, 10 million tons were cut, but poor organization, inefficiency, and inadequate transport prevented them from being processed. Machinery, replacement parts, and cement for construction often never left docks or storage depots. Quantities of cut sugar were not delivered to the *centrales*. In addition to the failure to bring in the harvest, there was the sharp dislocation of production resulting from the distorted effort pumped into a single sector of the economy.

Reasons for Cuba's Production Problems

The failure of the "Heroic Effort" has generated an interesting divergence of views of the reasons for Cuba's production problems. K. S. Karol's skeptical prescience of the harvest maintains that the insufficient output of Cuba's labor force was because the "relationship between man and society remains defective, not to say bad." Karol feels that there is a "striking contrast between hopes and reality." He supports his indictment by citing failures to overcome prerevolutionary atavisms such as great income differentials and the existence of luxury hotels and restaurants in Havana to soak up this excess income. He points to the existence of what he calls "socialist inflation," i.e., high demand and low supply, the long lines for short supplies, and inefficient distribution. Certain manipulators and hustlers are able to obtain scarce goods while the less aggressive did without. These charges are very interesting. If they are true, the revolution would seem to be losing its most crucial battle, the battle to destroy the old consciousness and build the new man. Karol sees the Cuban revolution, unlike the Chinese revolution to which he is partisan, as falling into the gray stagnation of the East European Soviet satellites.[22]

Karol's accurate predictions of Cuban economic failures notwithstanding, a number of failings in his analysis and the reports of other equally astute observers seem to contradict his cynical appraisal and exhume the possibility that Cuba is still in the process of creating a new socialist consciousness.

For one thing, Karol fails to demonstrate a causal nexus between shortages, low per capita output, inequalities, and lack of conformity to his political preferences. It would appear that Karol would want one to believe that the shortcomings he indicates cause a lowering of morale which in turn causes low output and this triad has negatively spiraling possibilities.

Second of all, most of his examples of inequalities and nonrevolutionary behavior were observed in Havana, an urban, bourgeois outpost in a country whose revolutionary thrust is in the countryside. People knowledgeable about Cuba note that the revolution intensifies as one travels east toward Oriente. One suspects that it was Karol's own urban inclinations that made Havana so important and the *campo* secondary in his observations of Cuban life.

Authors such as Fagen, Lockwood, and Zeitlin all demonstrate the very high morale and revolutionary enthusiasm of the Cuban people. It was not low morale and lack of consciousness that brought Cubans by the thousands into the fields during the torrid summer to voluntarily cut cane. Young Americans who joined the Venceremos Brigades told this writer how their own revolutionary fervor was ignited by the Cuban field workers with whom they cut cane. Some of these middle-class North Americans were amazed at the level of political analysis, the dedication, and the cooperative ability of people they termed simple *macheteros.*

Castro's own appraisal of Cuban economic shortcomings both contradict and in a sense confirm Karol's criticisms. Castro blames low output on underdevelopment. Underdevelopment manifests itself not only in material ways but also and most tellingly in the minds of the people. The Cuban leader characterizes one aspect of the problem this way:

> We are a people filled with enthusiasm and resolve, who at crucial
> moments are willing to lay down our lives, any hour, any day, anxious ·

to perform the most heroic deeds at any minute. But we are also a people lacking in constancy and courage, not at dramatic moments, but during each and every humdrum day. In other words we still lack persistence and are somewhat fickle in our heroism.[23]

Castro is here reporting a common characteristic of Latin Catholic culture. It is found throughout Latin America, mirrored in the exaltation of the transcendental act of the martyr and the hero. Remember the difficulty the old P.S.P. had in relating to the "adventurism" of some of its own young militants and to Castro's daring.

If we couple this tendency to be daring but not diligent with the problem Guevara called "absolute subjectivism," what remains in the dust is a destructive nonrelationship between the masses' inability and the leaders' shortsightedness. The giant *zafra* seems to be another case of the leaders' romantic desire to impose their will with little support in reality and make that reality conform to their will.

The failure of the giant *zafra* may have convinced Castro of the importance of the relationship between the leaders and the masses. Guevara, in "Man and Socialism in Cuba," refers to

. . . that close dialectical unity which exists between the individual and the mass, in which both are interrelated, and the mass, as a whole composed of individuals, is in turn interrelated with the leader.[24]

Castro mentions the lack of this "dialectical unity" in discussing the failures of the economy. Here he calls for a new way of integrating society. He gives an example of innovation in the way a factory should be run:

We don't believe that the problems of managing a plant should fall exclusively to the manager. It would really be worthwhile to begin introducing a number of new ideas. There should be a manager, naturally, for there must always be someone accountable, but we must begin to establish a collective body in the management of each plant. A collective body! It should be headed by one man, but it should also be made up of representatives of the advance workers' movement, the Young Communist League, the Party, and the Women's Front, if such a front can be organized within the plant.[25]

Later in the same speech, Castro asks,

Why should a manager have to be absolutely in charge? Why shouldn't we begin to introduce representatives of the factory's workers into its management? Why not have confidence? Why not put our trust in the tremendous proletarian spirit of man? . . .[26]

Having been separated from the people by his own subjectivity, Castro now states, "An effort of subjective character—we were saying—has to be made by all the people."[27] He is here suggesting that the greatest involvement of the people in the decisions they have to carry out is an attack on underdevelopment. He has called for the democratization of all institutions in the country. In July of 1970, he thought that it was enough to rely on the decisions of the Organization of Advanced Workers and other party-related organizations. As of that date, the main body of workers in a plant were still not involved in industrial decisions. Most recently, democracy has been expanded in the revivification of the trade union movement, which had been largely neglected and almost moribund. In September of 1970, Castro told a conference of the Trade Union Federation of Havana:

> Let us have faith in our workers and speedily carry out elections in all our trade unions . . . in an absolutely free way in which the workers nominate anyone they want. . . . Let us begin to democratize the labor movement. If it isn't democratic, it isn't worth anything.[28]

Castro's July 26, 1971, speech indicates that what has been called the "mass line," the vitalization of the workers' movement and other mass organizations, is now the focus of the revolutionary process. "We will continue to carry out the workers' assemblies, the discussions with the workers of the difficulties and the search for solutions."[29]

A central tenet of Marxist practice is that failure is more valuable in certain respects than success. The sugar may indeed have been a great failure. But in Marxist terms, it may have been a fruitful failure. Castro told the Cuban people that out of this failure shall grow triumph. A climactic triumph for the Cuban revolution would be the attainment of a take-off position in the struggle against underdevelopment. Since the most formidable enemy in this struggle is the subjective one, the old consciousness, a triumph over underdevelopment implies the growth of the new consciousness. For all the economic mishaps of the revolution, the Cuban militants seem to be continuing, experimenting, failing, and succeeding in this struggle.

Conclusion

European and North American critics have been vocally concerned about Cuba's politics—the alleged "Stalinization" of the revolution, the increased dependency on Soviet technical aid, and the stringency of laws and penalties for malingering. Problems arising from underdevelopment are left to those who must live with them, and the expansion of organizational experimentation and industrial democracy are ignored by non-third-world critics.

In conclusion, Cuba's revolution now stands face to face with its past. The old values of personalism, martyrdom, and what Guevara has called "absolute subjectivism" were the imperfect vehicles which have transported Cuba to its present. The next few years will tell us whether that present, with its consciousness of past error and future possibilities, will actually develop into something new and dynamic or whether it will stagnate in the pursuit of static goals.

NOTES TO CHAPTER 6

1. Irving Louis Horowitz, "Introduction: The Norm of Illegitimacy: The Political Sociology of Latin America" in *Latin American Radicalism,* ed. Irving Louis Horowitz et. al. (New York: Vintage Books, 1969), p. 5.
2. Enrique Jose Varona, quoted in Wyatt MacGaffey and Clifford R. Barnett, *Twentieth Century Cuba* (Garden City, New York: Anchor Books, 1965), p. 260.
3. John Gillin, *Twentieth Century Cuba,* p. 261.
4. Maurice Zeitlin, "Cuba: Revolution without a Blueprint," *Transaction* VI, No. 6 (April 1969): 38. For another elaboration of this point of view, see James O'Connor, *Origins of Socialism in Cuba* (Ithaca, New York: Cornell University Press, 1970).
5. Zeitlin, "Revolution without a Blueprint," p. 41.
6. *Ibid.*
7. Fidel Castro, Speech of July 26, 1970, published in *Granma,* August 2, 1970.
8. Jose Martí, Quoted in N. R. Duncan and J. N. Goodsel, *The Quest for Change in Latin America* (New York: Oxford University Press, 1970), p. 1.
9. Fidel Castro, *History Will Absolve Me* (New York: Lyle Stuart, 1961) pp. 37–38.
10. Hugh Thomas, "Middle Class Politics and the Cuban Revolution," in *The Politics of Conformity in Latin America,* ed. Claudio Veliz (London: Oxford University Press, 1970), pp. 259–60.
11. Manuel Urrutia, quoted in Herbert Matthews, *Fidel Castro* (New York: Simon & Schuster, 1969), p. 137.
12. Lopez-Fresquet, quoted in *Fidel Castro,* p. 137.
13. *Foco* as referred to here means a center of rural guerrilla activity. In the *foco* method of revolutionary insurrection, politics and party are to develop out of armed struggle as opposed to armed struggle emerging out of the politics of a vanguard party. For the best elaboration of the *foco* method, see Regis Debray, "Revolution in the Revolution?" *Monthly Review* XX, No. 3 (July-August 1967).
14. K. S. Karol, *Guerrillas in Power,* trans. Arnold Pomerans (New York: Hill and Wang, 1970), p. 64.
15. Fidel Castro, Radio and television broadcast of March 26, 1962, reprinted in *El Mundo* (Havana), March 27, 1962, translated and quoted in *Political Power in Latin America: Seven Confrontations,* ed. Richard R. Fagen and Wayne A. Cornelius, Jr. (Englewood Cliffs, New Jersey; Prentice-Hall, 1970).
16. Guevara, speech delivered before a seminar on planning, published in *Revolución* No. 2. (October 1963), translated and quoted in *Venceremos,* ed. John Gerassi (New York: Simon & Schuster, 1969), p. 260.
17. Guevara, in *Venceremos,* pp. 260–61.

18. Fidel Castro, speech of January 24, 1964, published in leaflet form in *Obra Revolucionaria* No. 3 (Havana, 1964): 16, quoted in *Guerrillas in Power,* pp. 407–8.

19. Fidel Castro, speech of June 19, 1963, *Obra Revolucionaria,* No. 15 (Havana 1963): 37, quoted in *Guerrillas in Power,* p. 411.

20. Joseph Kahl tells us that *conciencia* is a merger of consciousness, conscience, conscientiousness, and commitment. It is one of the most often used words in Cuba's vocabulary of revolution. Joseph A. Kahl, "The Moral Economy of a Revolutionary Society," *Transaction* VI, No. 6 (April 1969): 38.

21. Karol, *Guerillas in Power,* p. 410.

22. Ibid., p. 428.

23. Fidel Castro, speech to the Trade Union Congress, August 1966, translated and quoted in *Guerillas in Power,* pp. 426–71.

24. Guevara, translated and quoted in *Guerillas in Power,* p. 389.

25. Fidel Castro, speech of July 26, 1970, published in *Granma,* August 2, 1970.

26. *Ibid.*

27. *Ibid.*

28. Fidel Castro, translated and quoted in Lionel Martin, "Cuban Trade Union Overhaul," *Direct From Cuba* (Havana) No. 30 (December 15–30, 1970): 1.

29. Fidel Castro, translated and quoted by Lionel Martin, "July 26th Rally in Cuba," *Guardian* (New York), August 4, 1971, p. 12.

7
Conclusions

This work has treated the contribution of Catholic beliefs and values to the ideological superstructure of three Latin societies: Mexico, Chile, and Cuba. Common to these societies was the long rule of the Spanish imperium, rationalized in all of its exploitive and oppressive acts by the security of God's sanction. When Spain, too weak to defend its conquest, was ejected from the hemisphere by the creole oligarchy, Catholicism remained one of the important ideological forces through which an exploitive and oppressive hierarchy was perpetuated.

I do not hold here that the Latin ideology was ever purely Catholic. The Latin ideology has had, and still has, many strains and tints. Nineteenth-century commercial and industrial barons made their fortunes under the banner of liberalism and flew that banner over all of Latin America. Liberalism originated in Europe as the ideological companion of the commercial and industrial revolutions. Liberalism trumpeted the virtues of individualism, competition, and limited government interference in the economic and social life of a society. In Europe it countered the feudal notions of community and the responsibility of the prince for the relations and well-being of his subjects. In nineteenth-century Latin America, the newly incumbent commercial sectors selectively adapted liberalism. While they protected their monopolies with governmental power, they used the double-edged sword of laissez-faire economics and Darwinistic individualism, sliced the mantle of Catholic communal protection away from the Indian lands and villages. The liberal slogan was "each man for himself," rich Creole as well as poor Indian, in the struggle for survival. The result was pillage of the poor, great inroads against the power of the land, and the restructuring of Latin society. However, despite the strength of this liberal thrust, it did not erase nor did it have to erase all the Catholic elements of the dominant ideology.

Just as this book is not meant to ignore or discount the "Liberal Period" in Latin history, neither is it an attempt to denigrate the importance of the positivist rape of the people. Positivism emerged strongly in nineteenth-century Europe. It held that the problems of society could be resolved through the application of scientific analyses and methods. These methods were by definition above the chaos of political combat. To the liberal oligarchs, positivism had the allure of dispassionate efficiency and the benefit of rationalizing one's political opponents out of the picture. It should not be forgotten that Porfirio Díaz ruled Mexico for thirty years as a positivist apostle of the Frenchman Auguste Comte. It was a seemingly slavish adoration of the "higher" European culture which rationalized the sale of Mexico to European and North American capitalists. Positivism was the "'apolitical" key to wielding power by which the *científicos,* all above politics, stole from the poor in the name of the new religion of Science.

Liberalism has lost its thrust as a result of the Latin monopolists' desire for government protection and the limitations placed on national capitalist expansion by the economic domination of the United States. That tower of nonsense called positivism was partially destroyed in the Mexican revolutionary struggle. Positivism makes a pious appearance from time to time when groups of self-righteous plutocrats try to sell the people the austere benefits of "apolitical" rule. Jorge Alessandri's pristine rule of stagnation and dependency was one short-lived example of this attempt to govern "above politics." This former Chilean president filled his first cabinet in 1958 with a group of old conservatives who were presented to the nation as men above politics. The very political Chilean legislature rebelled and Alessandri was eventually forced into a more workable political arrangement. He fired his *científicos* and formed a cabinet which was more representative of the parties in the legislature. Although there is still nostalgia for the apolitical "man of respect" in Chile, Alessandri's defeat in the 1970 presidential election is partially an indication of the dying strength of that nostalgia. Although liberalism and positivism as well as other strong ideological currents once accompanied Catholicism as important parts of the Latin American superstructure, they have faded, while strong elements of Catholicism as a dually religious and secular set of beliefs and values has endured. It is the nature of this endurance that has been the subject of this work.

Although I have emphasized values, I have not meant to support the idealist argument of value determinism which holds that a society's organization follows initially from its values. I believe that a society's values emerge from the way the society organizes itself to survive. I also believe that even when values seem to have a life of their own, apparently divorced from the economic base from which they emerged, they ultimately reflect this economic organization of society. However, I am dismayed by a mechanistic economic determinism which sees values as well as other dominant institutions of a society as the instantaneous and immediate product of the dominant mode of production and somehow, as a result, the easy tool of the ruling class. This mechanistic argument states that the superstructure is at the mercy of the ruling class and can be abandoned or reinvigorated as this class desires. Engels criticizes this simplistic line in the following sentences:

> According to the materialist conception of history, the *ultimately* determining element in history is the production and reproduction of

real life. More than this neither Marx nor I have ever asserted. Hence if somebody twists this into saying that the economic element is the *only* determining one, he transforms that proposition into a meaningless, abstract, senseless phrase. The economic situation is the basis, but the various elements of the superstructure: political forms of the class struggle and its results, to wit: constitutions established by the victorious class after a successful battle, etc., juridical forms, and then even the reflexes of all these actual struggles in the brains of the participants, political, juristic, philosophical theories, religious views and their further development into systems of dogmas, also exercise their influence upon the course of the historical struggles and in many cases preponderate in determining their *form*. There is an interaction of all these elements in which, amid all the endless host of accidents (that is of things and events, whose inner connection is so remote or so impossible of proof that we can regard it as non-existent as negligible) the economic movement finally asserts itself as necessary. Otherwise, the application of the theory to any period of history one chose would be easier than the solution of a simple equation of the first degree.[1]

The focus of this book then, has been the continued existence in Latin America of a particular structure of values—those first synthesized in their-teenth-century Catholic Europe—and the integration of these values with a capitalist mode of production. I do not pretend to have solved in these pages the problem of the relationship between economic base and dominant ideology. The search for this solution is being pursued by scholars like Louis Althusser,[2] who builds on the works of Marx, Engels, and Gramsci. What I have done is to emphasize the uneven and atavistic relationship between the Latin American world view and the reality of the Latin economic systems —colonial, non-colonial, and Marxist revolutionary—especially in Chile and Cuba.

Let me advise the reader that although the Church and Catholic values have been cast in a very negative light here, I believe that today the Latin Church is going through what may be a mortal struggle in which progressive revolutionary clergy and laymen are battling the heretofore triumphant reactionary elements whose existence has been based on the survival of oligarchy and foreign domination. Unfortunately this book, in its present form, cannot do justice to the movement of revolutionary Christianity in Latin America. I plan to investigate and document this struggle in a future book. At present I can merely point to the emergence of a "Theology of Liberation" which is a new and progressive response to intensifying contradictions between imperialism and its colonized people.

[1] Friedrich Engels, Letter to Joseph Bloch, London, September 21–22, 1890.
[2] *For Marx* (New York: Pantheon Books, 1969).

Postscript

This postscript is by no means a definitive analysis nor a detailed chronicle of the events which led up to and followed the tragic death of Salvador Allende Gossens and the destruction of constitutional government in Chile. It is merely an attempt to place those events within the purview of this book: the historical interplay between Catholic values, ideas, and formulae and the class conflict which have marked the calendar of Latin America's development.

The *golpe de estado* of September 11, 1973 destroyed both the government of Chile and its ancient formula of Thomistic legalism. At 11:30 A.M. of that winter Tuesday, tanks, troops, and planes of the Chilean armed forces, faced with Salvador Allende's repudiation of their surrender ultimatum, reduced the presidential palace to an ashen smoking shell and the president to a bullet-riddled corpse. With equally relentless force and fire they destroyed popular resistance and thrust a military junta into the role of arbiter of Chilean life. While proclaiming the repressive restrictions of a state of siege, the leader of the junta, General Augosto Pinochet Ugarte, declared the end of politics in Chile. Marxist political groupings, including Allende's Socialists, the Communist Party, MAPU, and another splinter group, were summarily outlawed. Opposition leaders, and opponents of the new order were killed, arrested, or fled to exile. The dismissed and destroyed U.P. coalition was accused of having led the country into chaos, of having been corrupt, of having imported 10,000 foreign extremists into Chile, and of having planned the assassination of opposition leaders. A white paper detailing the "crimes of the Allende era" was promised. The world was told that President Allende had committed suicide rather than face the tribunal of Chilean justice. In summary the armed forces did what the Marxists would not—they destroyed the pride of Chilean political tradition: peaceful succession, lawful procedure, and constitutional pluralistic democracy. By bullet, bomb, and decree, they categorically disenfranchised Chile's Marxists and left the franchise in limbo for all others.

While, for reasons we shall discuss, Chilean legalism is dead, its rhetoric has yet to be interred. On September 21, General Pinochet remarked, "This is a Chilean movement [referring to the military takeover]. Chile's citizens are legalistic, and even in a state of siege [such as now], we are using the laws. They may be military laws, but they are still laws."[1]

Another member of the junta, Air Force General Gustavo Leigh, said shortly after that the junta has requested the nation's constitutional law professors to help to draft a new constitution "that will give participation to all Chileans, including workers, peasants, guilds, technicians, and women."[2]

Gustavo Leigh "want[s] to leave a new base for the citizens to better choose the government they want."[3] Leigh was explicit in this raw appeal to legalism that Chile's political parties would have no part in drafting the new constitution.

With these references to Chilean legalism and the need for a new constitutional formula, the generals bring to mind two old but important elements of the Chilean political heritage. Both, I believe, are anachronistic. The first is an appeal to *Derecho.*[4] The second, referring to the role of constitutional law professors and the exclusion of politicians, exhumes the spectre of positivism.

As I noted in chapter 3, *el Derecho* as opposed to *las leyes* is the higher context of law which articulates with natural law within which the society should ideally be organized. The golpe, in essence, was called forth by the disharmony between *las leyes,* emanating from the constitution of 1925, and *el Derecho,* the ideal formula for rational organization. Here positivism intrudes itself in the form of "apolitical" legalists, i.e., constitutional law professors, above the mundane melee of party politics, who will "scientifically" construct the new formula which will reintegrate *las leyes* with *el Derecho.* As a result the people will be given their proper political organization. The constitutionalists of 1833 and 1925 were obviously able to discover such formulae. Today, I believe, the situation is different: *el Derecho* is out of reach and the positivist solution, always a conservative ideal, never real, is especially unrealistic now.

The manner of Allende's rise and the nature of his fall underscore the reality of Chilean social disharmony and the necessity of a resolution which is supremely political in that it must deal with the questions of power and intensified class conflict. Although the army was the body that smashed the stones of the Thomistic fortress, class conflict was the soul of this assault. Allende's incumbency and the short reign of the *Unidad Popular* both expressed and heightened the contradictions of more than a century of the evolution of this conflict. The 44 percent plurality enjoyed by the U.P. in the 1972 congressional elections, the mass worker demonstrations in favor of the Marxist parties, the success (limited though it was) of groups like the MIR (Movement of the Revolutionary Left) among slum dwellers and peasants, must be looked at in the context of that development; so must the intense and prolonged battle of the middle class against the possibility of a socialist Chile. Within the space limitations of this postscript I should like to present a brief outline of the development of class consciousness in Chile, to dispel the notion that civil chaos in Chile is ahistorical and can be resolved by an apolitical legalist constitutional formula.

Although the nineteenth century was dominated by the oligarchic and authoritistic constitution of 1833, it was also marked by the entry of the new middle sectors and the popular classes onto the stage of history.

In 1850 Francisco Bilbao began the process of politicizing the working class, when he organized the *Sociedad de la Igualdad* (Society of Equality). This body was joined by a large number of workers who campaigned for freedom of suffrage and civil liberties. This was the first workers' challenge to the long-dominant oligarchy. The end of the century was marked by the forward movement of organizations such as the Workers Social Center (1896), the Socialist Union (1897), and the Francisco Bilbao Worker's Party (1898). Federico Gil relates that "newspapers such as *The Worker, The Proletarian, The People,* although ephemeral, were among the early interpreters of the Chilean Populist Movement."[5]

The consciousness first manifested in these nineteenth-century organizations was intensified by the labor unrest and corresponding repression that marked the first two decades of the twentieth century. In 1907, 2,000 nitrate workers were senselessly massacred in Iquique. In Puerto Natales in 1919, and again in Magallanes in 1920, equally tragic repression took place. Here the working class received its primary lessons about the ruling elite's desire to crush social unrest. In this context Luis Emilio Recabarren founded the 1912 Worker's Socialist Party. This organization was to become the Chilean Communist Party when some years later Recabarren led it into the Commintern of the Third International. Thus Chilean Marxism was born early and internationalized.

The fourteen-day Chilean Socialist Republic proclaimed by Marmeduke Grove in 1932 nationalized Chilean socialism and in a sense wed Salvador Allende to the development of the workers' movement. In 1933, inspired partly by the events of the preceding year and partly by the Moscow line of the Chilean Communist Party, Allende helped to found the Chilean Socialist Party. This party was to be more nationalist and more revolutionary than its Communist compatriot. These events, reaching back into the struggles and organizations of the nineteenth century, set the stage for the precipitous moments of the 1970s. One should not forget that the Chilean popular movements were all informed and invigorated by a world context which witnessed the triumph of socialism in Russia, China, and Cuba. In addition the Chilean popular classes shared the knowledge of a third world in foment and revolution.

This development of popular organization and consciousness was complemented and ultimately contradicted by the intensified politicization of the Chilean middle class. This social grouping, unlike its counterparts in many Latin American countries, has become a class for, and of, itself. The self-conscious thrust of this class was molded by its political struggles in the nineteenth century against the ultramontane oligarchy and most lately against the threat of popular class domination. The middle class fought its first battles through the medium of the Radical Party. The Radicals, inspired by free masonry, were a grouping of professionals, white collar workers, various mine owners, and lower middle class tradesmen. Although this class first organized itself politically in the nineteenth century, it won its first electoral victory within the Liberal Alliance of Radicals and Democrats behind the candidacy of Arturo Alessandri in 1920. This was a seminal victory because it gave the nonoligarchic middle class a hand in writing the successful constitution of 1925.

In 1938 these two lines of development, of the popular class and the middle class, converged in the victory of the Popular Front. This was the coalition of Socialists, Communists, and Radicals which elected the Radical, Pedro Aguirre Cerda, to the presidency. Ten years later, the Radical President Gonzales Videla was to turn on his former working class allies in the repressive "Law for the Defense of Democracy" which outlawed the Communist Party. Although the Radicals were among the first and most important middle class organizations, the Christian Democrats provided a latter-day bridge between the middle class and the oligarchy. The group, first calling itself the National Falange in the late 1930s, emerged out of dissatisfaction with the antiquated Conservative Party. Christian Democrats see the solution of Chile's ills in what they call the "Communitarian Society." They wish to maintain social hierarchy, class harmony, and democracy at once. They promised a "Revolution in Liberty." Along with its former partisans in the oligarchic Liberal and Conservative parties, Christian Democracy did much to alert the middle class to the "evils of Marxism." It used the bogeymen of the Soviet and Cuban revolutions to gather the biggest electoral victory in Chilean history in 1964. Under the banner of Christian Democracy, all elements of the middle class hoped to find social justice for themselves while not having to experience the social dislocations and sacrifices called for by socialist revolution. Here the *nouveau riche* would find protection and the not-yet-successful would discover deliverance through the medium of political power.

It should be remembered that all these political convergences and divergences, parties, and elections occurred under the overriding aegis of legalism and constitutionalism. Under this aegis, Salvador Allende came to power in 1970 with 36.8 percent of the vote. His victory placed the working class center stage to make fundamental change without the mandate of the majority. His coalition was rent by uneasy alliance and divergence of views. The Communists were conciliatory and, after initial reforms, wanted the slow procedure of consolidation. Many of Allende's Socialists wanted accelerated revolutionary moves. The MIR, partially behind the government and partially reserved, pushed the expropriation of farm and factory. The groupings that Allende navigated were hardly a revolutionary phalanx of solidarity.

The U.P. never commanded a majority of the Congress. The opposition,

consisting of Christian Democrats and Nationalists, voiced and exacerbated
the fears and recalcitrance of their middle class and oligarchic electoral
base.

The difficulties of the U.P. were anticipated by events and activities that
followed Allende's election but preceded his inauguration. Almost immediately following the U.P. triumph, the Army commander, René Schneider,
loyal to Allende, was assassinated by a right wing terror unit. This act
commenced Allende's woes. Capital began to leave the country in increased
volume. Investors, fearing nationalization, withheld further investment. An
already underutilized productive capacity suffered further slowdowns.
Farmers killed their pregnant cows and their bulls. They feared the seizure
of their land and did not plant.

Among Allende's first acts was freezing prices and raising wages. This
immediately strained the always narrow consumer market. Shortages occurred. This situation worsened as producers and distributors withheld
goods from the market, further curtailed production, and called strikes.
Those who could get goods, hoarded. Black marketeering became the normal mechandising procedure. The last year of Allende's presidency witnessed an inflation rate of 300 percent.

This catalogue of woes was worsened by right wing terror tactics of
sabotage, assassination, and violent street demonstrations.

Allende's supporters and those to the left of him accelerated worker and
peasant takeovers, attacks on black-marketeers, and giant mass street demonstrations of their own.

The United States contributed to Chile's tribulations by building an
"invisible wall" around the country. In order to begin building a new society
Chile needed capital. The United States, antagonistic to Marxist success,
and chafing over the nationalization of its copper holdings, saw to it that
Chile's credit lines were severed. While halting all other aid, the United
States continued to finance Chile's army, granting more than 14 million
dollars in aid during Allende's incumbency. How many more dollars
financed agitation and subversion is, at this date, a subject of contention.
The collusion among the CIA, American corporations, and the Chilean
right no doubt will be subject to much investigation and conjecture.

Allende's legalistic formulae could neither resolve nor contain the antagonism of these contradictions. However, in spite of cataclysmic problems,
Allende's government did manage accomplishments in three areas. It nationalized copper, broke the back of the *latifundia* system, and nationalized
500 corporations. These achievements are very tenuous at this time, as the
generals decide the fate of nationalized property. As Allende's fall ap-
proached, his attempts to rule dissolved into futile Machiavellian gestures.
Faced with a national truck owner-driver strike, strikes by physicians, airline
pilots, and shopkeepers, demands by the opposition for a military cabinet,
Allende formed and reformed governments. He formed cabinets with mili-

tary men and without. At the end nothing seemed to work. The popular classes were insistent on their revolution and the middle class more insistently and more powerfully bent on stopping it.

There is no predetermined victor in this struggle, but it has become clear that no legalistic formula can resolve it. It is also difficult to believe that terror and repression can totally destroy the very broad popular class development of more than a century. At best, the future seems to hold civil disorder; at worst, the fraternal destruction of civil war.

The army, taking power in a devastatingly bloody coup, has transformed its role in Chilean history. It is no longer the professional guardian of the constitution. It has become an arbiter in the conflict of the classes. Now powerful, seemingly unified in command on the side of the bourgeoisie, tomorrow it may be split, smashing against itself on both sides of a civil struggle. The generals' call for a new constitution seems a nostalgic joke, not a reference to the future.

NOTES TO POSTSCRIPT

1. Los Angeles Times, September 22, 1973, Part 1, p. 3.
2. Los Angeles Times, September 23, 1973, Part 1, p. 5.
3. *Ibid.*
4. See Chapter 3 above, especially p. 26.
5. Frederico G. Gil, The Political System of Chile (Boston: Houghton Mifflin Company, 1966). p. 54.

Index